The Third Experiment

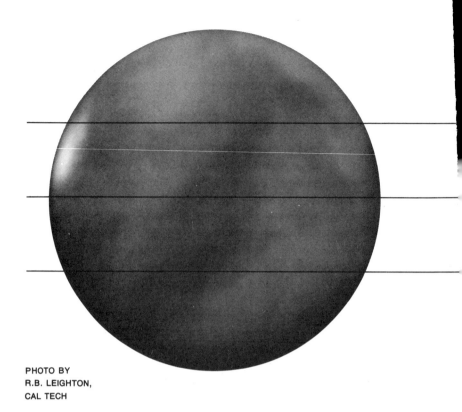

ILLUSTRATED WITH PHOTOGRAPHS,
DRAWINGS AND DIAGRAMS

THE

THIRD

EXPERIMENT

Is There Life on Mars?

DAVID E. FISHER

ATHENEUM   New York   1985

Library of Congress Cataloging in Publication Data

Fisher, David E.
The third experiment

Bibliography.
Includes index.
SUMMARY: Traces the history of scientific and
imaginative thought about life on the planet Mars, and
analyzes three experiments included in the Viking mission
to Mars intended to determine whether or not the planet
could support life.
1. Mars (planet)—Juvenile literature. 2. Life on
other planets—Juvenile literature. [1. Mars-(planet)
2. Life on other planets. 3. Viking Mars Program]
I. Title.
QB641.F53 1985   574.999'23   84-21548
ISBN 0-689-31080-3

This book is gratefully dedicated to
Ms. Zola Mae Blakeslee,
the world's greatest librarian . . .
And to all other librarians,
wherever you are.

Contents

PART I

MARS!

*I have always looked on
myself as some sort of
Martian.*

—RAY BRADBURY

CHAPTER 1

The Beginning

IT WAS on Halloween, October 31, 1938, that the Martians attacked.

There were no regular television broadcasts in those days, and most people spent their evenings cozily listening to the radio. That evening millions of people tuned in to CBS and heard the music of a dance band, playing swing from a ballroom in New York. The music was interrupted by a news bulletin, reporting that strange flashes of light, perhaps explosions, had been seen on the planet Mars. A later news bulletin told them that something strange was happening in New Jersey: cylinders of unknown origin had crashed in a farmfield near Princeton. Updated bulletins began arriving with increasing frequency and increasing excitement as the cylinders opened and strange beings crawled out. The police were being summoned, the army was arriving—the creatures destroyed them with strange weapons! The cylinders were space vehicles carrying an invading army of Martians!

Many of the people listening had tuned in too late to hear the opening announcement of the program, that it was a production of the CBS Mercury Theatre of the Air, presenting a dramatization of the novel by H.G. Wells, *The War of the*

Worlds. These people thought they were hearing real news bulletins, and they believed them. The roads leading out of New Jersey became crowded that night with people fleeing the invasion of the Martians, fleeing for their lives from the rampaging monsters, spurred on by the unceasing radio bulletins that they listened to while they drove as fast as they could.

Why? Why did people, grown-up, mature adults, believe such nonsense? Did they really believe that slithering, fantastically grotesque serpent-creatures actually lived on Mars and had created a civilization so much greater and more advanced than our own that they could soar in incredible space ships through the empty skies to Earth, and that they could destroy our armies with weapons we could only dream about?

The answer lies in Mars itself and in the stories earthmen had been telling themselves about the distant red planet ever since the first scientific discoveries had shown that Mars was a planet very similar to Earth. If life had formed and flourished on Earth, then why not on Mars?

CHAPTER 2

Before the Beginning

IF YOU go out at night and "look up in perfect silence at the stars," as everyone should do whenever we get a chance to get away from the glare of city lights, you are bound to feel a wonderful sense of awe at the beauty of the universe—and that's about all you're going to get out of it. I'm not knocking that feeling, it's worth a lot, particularly when you're disappointed in love or worried about the future of mankind in a nuclear age or aggravated by your parents or your children, but it's not enough. If you have any intelligence you want more than a feeling of awe: you want to understand what it's all about. And for that you have to do more than stand out there gawking at the stars.

Galileo Galilei was one of the first to do more. He looked at the stars, all right, but he looked at them through a telescope. In 1610 he was the first person to do this, or at least the first person to understand what he saw and to tell the world about it. And what he saw was that some of the stars, which the ancient Greeks had called the "wandering stars," weren't stars at all. Practically all of the stars in the sky, when looked at through the telescope, didn't change their appearance at all: they still looked like bright points of light, and nothing else. But

5

the "wandering stars" (the Greek word for that is *planets*) changed their shape under the telescope: instead of simply being bright points, Galileo could see that they were instead round disks. Furthermore, he could see the characteristics of their light change as they moved around the sun. From these observations he concluded correctly that while the normal stars are objects like the sun—flaming balls of gaseous fires—the wandering stars, the planets, are spheres that travel (like the earth) around the sun and (again like the earth) have no light of their own but only reflect the sunlight from their surface. In fact, he concluded, the planets are other worlds, similar to the earth; they are not stars at all.

Galileo's work helped establish the Copernican Revolution in men's minds: named after Nicholas Copernicus, a Polish astronomer and philosopher, the revolution overthrew the old ideas about the nature and structure of the universe. Until then, men had thought of the earth as the center of the universe, unique and alone as a place where things such as people might live. Somewhere up above, among or beyond the stars, was Heaven; somewhere vaguely "down below" was Hell. But now, in the middle of the seventeenth century, people began to understand that the earth was nothing more than another planet, one of nearly a dozen that circled the sun (*ellipsed* the sun, actually, but that sounds awkward).

With this realization of what the universe is really like—that we inhabit a ball of stone and water floating through space— came the first stretchings of our imagination, stretching to reach out to some of these other worlds. The first person to do so was the French poet and swordsman of nearly mythical prowess, Cyrano de Bergerac. In the 1650s he wrote of his travels to the sun and the moon by ingenious methods. He stood on a plate in a field of grass at night, and when dawn came and the dew under the plate evaporated and flew to heaven, it carried him along with it. Another method, as recounted by Edmond Rostand in his magnificent play about Cyrano, was by standing on a metal plate and throwing a magnet above him; the metal plate was lifted by the magnet's attraction, Cyrano caught the magnet, threw it up again, the metal plate was lifted farther, and so on by steps until he finally reached the moon.

With these stories we first began to lift our eyes beyond the horizons of earth and to wonder about what was out there in the vast, empty stretches of space. But our imaginations need a firm base on which to stand, we need to know something in order to imagine more, and so for the next two centuries all our thoughts about the wonders of space were focused on the scientific discoveries that came slowly but emphatically.

This book is about the merging of these two great facets of the human mind: imaginative fantasy and observational science. They came together in the most exciting scientific experiment ever undertaken, the search for life on another world. In order to understand how we ever had the *chutzpa* to reach our hands and minds out across more than two hundred million miles of space to touch another world and look for living creatures there, we have to first look at the background that was being built up over centuries.

What is Mars?

And why should we expect to find life there?

CHAPTER 3

Mars and Man

WE DON'T KNOW precisely where and precisely when mankind originated, but ever since we somehow developed a mind capable of recognizing that we exist, we had visualized the universe as being of two parts: "here" and "there".

"Here" was the world we inhabited, the land we walked on and the waters we sailed on and the air we breathed. "There" was everywhere else: the sun, moon, and stars. We didn't know what they were, but we knew they were *different*.

We knew that, that is, up until the middle of the seventeenth century. And then suddenly with the use of the telescope a few people began to claim that there were other worlds like ours floating around up there. In particular, Mars began to look a lot like Earth. Over the next two centuries a series of telescopic observations were made, and each one showed us that Mars was more and more like the earth.

In the year 1659, Christian Huygens, a Dutch scientist, made a telescope much better than Galileo's. He looked at Mars and saw dark patches, like those we see on the Moon. Thinking what the earth would look like if seen from outer space, he decided that these dark area must be oceans, and so named them with the Latin word *maria*.

A few years later, in 1666, Jean Domenique Cassini watched Mars hour after hour throughout the night and saw the dark maria revolving across the face of the sphere. Obviously Mars was spinning on its axis, just as the earth does, and in fact at almost precisely the same rate—twenty-four hours per revolution. So there must be days and nights on Mars, just as there are on earth. Furthermore, Cassini saw that the poles of Mars were white; he guessed that this meant that the planet has polar ice caps, again just like the earth.

Nothing new of any great importance was discovered about Mars for over a hundred years, and then in 1784 William Herschel, a German musician who was awarded the post of organist at the famous Octagon Chapel in Bath, England, and who had been looking through his own telescopes at the stars as a hobby, reported to the British Royal Society that he saw not only the polar ice caps and the dark maria, but also occasional patches of brightness that moved across the surface of the planet; these could be nothing else but clouds, which meant immediately that Mars had not only an atmosphere but rain—because clouds are moisture condensing in the air.

All of this made Mars so earthlike that Herschel rather casually concluded, and no one seems to have argued with him, that "Mars has a considerable but modest atmosphere, so that its inhabitants probably enjoy a situation in many respects similar to our own."

Now to appreciate the reasoning behind this statement, it's important to put our minds back to the world as it existed a couple of hundred years ago when Herschel was talking. Three hundred years before that, Columbus had sailed across the oceans and discovered a new land, and found that it was inhabited by a new race of humanity never known before. Twenty years after that, Magellan sailed across the Pacific and found it dotted with islands—and every large island was inhabited by people. In 1543, a Portugese sailing ship bound for China was

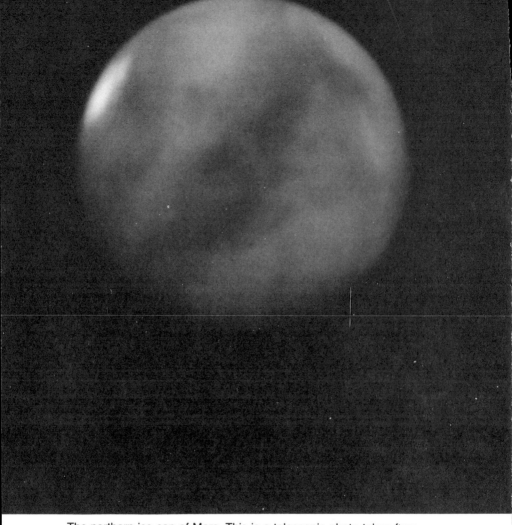

The northern ice cap of Mars. This is a telescopic photo taken from earth, using a twentieth century telescope. R.B. LEIGHTON, CAL TECH

blown off course by a violent storm, and when the sailors made landfall they found they were on a previously undiscovered island which was eventually named Japan—and again they found that this isolated island on the other side of the world was inhabited by mankind. In 1606, the Dutch explorer Willem Jansz and the Spaniard Luis de Torres independently found a gigantic island in the southern waters of the Pacific Ocean; it was named Australia and it too was peopled with a strange new race. In the desolate wastes of Alaska, Greenland and Iceland another race was discovered: the Eskimos.

It seemed that wherever man went, he found other men already there. It didn't matter how hot the new land was or how cold, how arid or how wet, how pleasant or how wild, somehow there seemed to be a new race of men for every spot on the globe.

And so when Herschel looked through his telescope and found that the new world of Mars had day and night, oceans and an atmosphere, wind and rain, it was perfectly natural to suppose that there too we would find a new race of mankind settled in and thriving.

They would be savages, of course, that went without saying. To the European mind of the eighteenth century everybody who was not a white Christian European was a savage; a poor, ignorant, humble human being in great need of spiritual salvation through Christ Jesus—and of course in great need of being economically exploited or even kidnapped and sold into slavery. The thought that the Martians might be creatures superior to us was an unChristian one that didn't enter anyone's mind for another hundred years—when the canals of Mars were discovered.

During these hundred years more people began to construct more and better telescopes with which to look at the mysterious planet. Some of these people began to think that they sometimes saw what appeared to be straight lines on the surface of the planet, many hundreds of miles long. In 1869, the papal astronomer at Rome, Father Pierre Angelo Secchi, used the Italian word *canali* (which translates as *channels*) to describe these lines. And a few years later this concept exploded in Milan.

Milan is a large city in northern Italy. Today it is not only the home of the world-famous La Scala Opera House, it is a typical commercial city of the modern world—crowded, dirty, and polluted. But in 1877 it was clean and lovely, and the Brera Observatory there was blessed with some of the best "seeing" in the world. (The term "seeing" is used by astronomers to describe the atmospheric conditions that affect telescopic observations: thus an observatory built on a mountaintop in a desert would peer out at the stars through clear, crisp air and would have excellent seeing, while someone trying to observe the skies from a basement window in Manhattan would experience abominable seeing.) The director of the Brera Observatory in 1877 was Giovanni Virginio Schiaparelli, and that brilliant summer in Italy the seeing was particularly good. Schiaparelli studied Mars on five especially good nights and saw the *canali* more clearly than anyone ever had.

When he reported the results of his observations to the Society of Italian Spectroscopists he interpreted the canali as rivers, linking the *maria* or seas. He even named them, many of them after the great rivers of the earth, such as the Euphrates. Mars by this time was beginning to look very much like the earth.

But there were problems. No one else, it seemed, could see the canals (as they were called by this time in English). For nearly another ten years Schiaparelli was the only person to see them when he looked at Mars. Then, in 1886, several other astronomers in England, France, and the United States claimed to see them, while other observers denied their existence.

How was this possible? Simply because the telescopes a hundred years ago were not very good: when people looked at Mars through them they saw a blurred image. The people who saw the canals claimed that they simply had better eyesight than those who couldn't see them; their antagonists claimed that those who saw the canals simply had a better imagination.

The controversy over the canals inspired a wealthy young American to leave his Boston family and build the world's best observatory in Flagstaff, Arizona. This man, Percival Lowell, went out there because the dry, clear air gave excellent seeing, and with the observatory he built he was able to get the clearest possible views of Mars. Did he see the canals?

You bet your life he did! He saw more canals, longer canals, and straighter canals than anyone before him ever had. They were, in fact, so long and so straight that he was quite certain they could not be natural rivers (as Schiaparelli had supposed). On the contrary, Lowell wrote in articles and books that the mistranslation of the Italian word *canali* into the English *canals* was a lucky one—for the canali really were canals laid out by intelligent Martians to irrigate the entire surface of their planet!

By this time it was known that although there was an atmosphere on Mars, it was much less than that on Earth; although there were clouds, there was much less rain than on earth. Mars was, in fact, as Lowell saw it, a drying, dying planet. Eons ago the Martians had had a flourishing civilization, but now they were in danger of their planet turning into one vast desert. And so they had built these planet-wide canals to irrigate their planet much as we do arid regions of our own country.

The engineering skills needed to create such a vast network boggle the imagination, but they didn't boggle Lowell's. It only proved to him that the Martians were an older, more technologically advanced race than we Earthlings. And his imagination took our own world by storm. Tennyson wrote:

If we lived on Mars and looked on earth. . . .
Could we dream of wars and carnage, craft and
  madness, lust and spite,
Roaring London, raving Paris, in that point of
  peaceful light?

The Martians could not see us or our cities, and we could not see them or theirs; but what a marvelous discovery to have seen their canals, and thus to know that they were up there!

And yet . . . other astronomers still could not see the canals. Fierce arguments raged, but Lowell's argument was always the same: he had the best telescope and the observatory with the best seeing in the world; if others couldn't see the canals, it was obviously because their equipment just wasn't good enough.

It was a good argument, and most people accepted it. In 1898 H.G. Wells wrote his classic novel, *The War of the Worlds,* on which the 1938 radio program was based, and everyone accepted it as a wonderful story *that could easily happen.* Nearly everyone, you see, accepted this vision of Mars as a planet harboring an advanced race, but a planet doomed to die. The idea that these creatures would attempt to find a home by conquering another planet made much sense. This period, from about 1895 to 1938, was the height of the belief in weird, intelligent creatures on Mars. In story after story we were introduced to variations on the theme, until it became nearly taken for granted that the Martians existed; we just weren't sure exactly what they looked like.

In one of the first and greatest series of stories about the planet, in fact, the Martians came in all shapes and sizes, a variety to fit each and every imagination. In 1912 Edgar Rice Burroughs, the creator of *Tarzan,* published in a cheap pulp magazine a short novel titled *Under the Moons of Mars.* This began the saga of Capt. John Carter, gentleman of Virginia, and his adventures on Mars. The story began when Carter, surrounded by angry Apache warriors and about to lose his scalp, lifted his eyes to the planet Mars and, somehow, by concentrating on it, managed to sort of dissolve his terrestrial body into an astral dimension and found that he was rematerialized far away from the rampaging Apaches—on the surface of Mars! This beginning was an exercise in pure imagination rather than science, but the rest of the book leaned heavily on what was really known about the planet—remembering, of course, that not very much was known and so there was still plenty of room for Burroughs's imagination to roam.

The planet Mars, as seen by Carter, as imagined by Burroughs, as visualized by Schiaperelli and Lowell, was an ancient planet, still vigorous but dying. A million years ago a mighty civilization had flourished there; a civilization of the kind we only dream about here on earth. A planet-wide system of world government was established, and the advanced humanlike race governed firmly but fairly over the lesser breeds without the law. But then, in keeping with the scientific observations that the atmosphere of Mars today is weak and vacuous, the oceans of Mars began to evaporate. The system of canals was built to irrigate the planet, but as the surface began to dry up, the established government was attacked and began to crumble under the onslaughts of a variety of half-savage, half-animal races. Parables can be drawn with the collapse of our own ancient Roman and Greek civilizations, when they were attacked by barbarian tribes from beyond their frontiers. On Mars the chief villains were the *tharks*, vaguely human in appearance but with green skin, four huge arms, and elephantlike tusks.

All of which was quite a shock to Capt. John Carter, but—anticipating Superman—he found that in the lighter gravity of Mars he could leap tremendous distances and had superhuman strength. And so he set to work on the side of truth and justice—which means of course on the side of the Martians that most resembled humans. But no sooner was he involved than he was captured by the tharks—who turned out to be not so awful after all, especially when compared with *their* enemies, the white-furred, four-armed apes! And so Carter goes from one adventure to another, finding romance along the way, marrying a princess of the humanoid Orovar race and becoming a father (well, sort of a father: the baby turns out to be an egg); then, before the egg hatches and we find out if it's a boy or a girl (or whatever) the same mysterious astral force that picked Carter up from among the Apaches and spirited him to Mars suddenly seizes him again and throws him back to earth!

Well! The reading public wasn't going to sit still for that, and so another book followed, and another after that, and for the next thirty years Captain Carter zoomed back and forth to Mars and kept two generations of schoolboys entertained—and along the way he stimulated the imaginations of a good number of these schoolboys who grew up to become the scientists who sent the first real rockets to Mars.

John Carter was the first, but not the last Earthling who discovered rich civilizations on the Mars of our imaginations. In 1928, a short novel by Phil Nowlan was published in *Amazing Stories*; it told about a pilot who was accidentally asphyxiated in a coal mine after crashing, and the strange vapors put him to sleep for five hundred years. His name was Buck Rogers, and he woke to a world where space travel was an accomplished fact, and where wars were fought with the people of other planets. Buck Rogers became one of the most famous people in the world, even though he was only imaginary. His adventures were found in books, magazines, on the radio and in the movies—although his movie career was cut short in 1941, when the Japanese attacked Pearl Harbor. Because, you see, in the movie Buck had scooted off to Saturn to recruit help for the earthlings who were being invaded by alien beings from another galaxy, and when the saviors from Saturn arrived they were yellow! We couldn't have America being saved by our yellow friends when we had to convince everyone that the Japanese were despicable beasts; and so the movie was removed from circulation, and I don't think it has ever been shown since.

Flash Gordon, on the other hand, went to Mars in another movie in 1938, and when he got there he found, of course, an advanced race of people. Other adventure stories followed these two, and you could hardly pick up a newspaper in those years without reading either in the comics or the movie pages about a new race of Martians who were up to something funny.

And then, in 1950, Ray Bradbury ushered in a new age of Martian fantasy with his poetic novel, *The Martian Chronicles.* His Mars was not a world of fantastic monsters and spine-tingling adventures for superheroes from Earth, but instead it was a world quite like our earth in the sense that it harbored a "Martian" humanity. Although the planet itself was weirdly ex- otic compared to earth—"They had a house of crystal pillars on the planet Mars by the edge of an empty sea, and every morn- ing you could see Mrs. K eating the golden fruits that grew from the crystal walls . . ."—the Martians themselves, despite their brown skins, yellow coin eyes, and soft musical voices, were re- cognizably human. So human, in fact, that they doubted the existence of life on other planets:

"Yll?" she called quietly. "Do you ever wonder if—well, if there *are* people living on the third planet?"

But Yll shook his head. "The third planet is incapable of supporting life," he said patiently.

All great works, like ships speeding across a calm sea, leave a spreading wake behind them. Into the wake left by *The Mar- tian Chronicles* swam a host of other science-fiction writers, and Mars blossomed into a real world with real, lifelike Martians;

the differences between them and earthlings only accentuated the similarities of their and our concerns with life and death and the worlds we live on. Ray Bradbury had almost single-handedly transformed science fiction into a serious literary endeavor.

But throughout these years, even as the stories of the Martians spread through our modern mythologies, people were still arguing about those canals. More and more people were building better and better observatories, and still nobody but Percival Lowell could see the canals. Other scientific observations began to come in, casting doubt on the idea of a civilized race on Mars.

The first of these observations was an attempt to measure the temperature on the planet. The only way to do this was to measure the heat it radiates out to earth, since we were at that time still stuck here on this planet two hundred million miles away. The heat received from an object depends on how warm it is, but also on how far away it is. For example, if you put your hand up against a normal light bulb it feels distinctly hot (while it's turned on, of course), but a few feet away from it you can't detect any heat. On the other hand, if you stand a few feet away from a burning building, you can feel that it's a bit hotter than a light bulb.

In 1907, a scientist named A.R. Wallace measured the temperature of Mars by constructing sensitive heat detectors and putting them at the focus of a large telescope. They were barely able to detect any heat at all. The detectors were nowhere near as sensitive as those we can make today, and the error in his results was large, but even after correcting for the effect of great distance the results showed that Mars was very cold. It was, in fact, below the freezing point of water. It was *always* below freezing, on the equator as well as the poles, in day as well as night. If the temperature is below freezing, then there is no liquid water on Mars, and therefore no use for anything like "canals".

Even worse, we had learned by then that no life can exist without liquid water. We are, you and I, essentially nothing but bags of water carried around in our skin, with a few other elements added. Without the presence of liquid water to carry these essential elements around, to allow them to interact in the complex chemistry that gives rise to life, there could be no life. None at all. And if the temperature on Mars is always below freezing, there is no water there; and therefore, there is no life there.

Then, in 1913, an English schoolteacher carried out the most ingenious of all the Mars experiments, and he did it without an observatory, without a telescope, without ever looking up at the skies. He simply took a large sheet of paper and printed on it an array of random dots, in no pattern at all. When this teacher (his name was E.W. Maunder) put this sheet of paper up against the blackboard in front of his classroom and asked the boys to write down what they saw, he got very interesting results. The boys up front could see the dots clearly, and unanimously they wrote that the paper carried simply a bunch of dots, with no pattern. The boys at the very back of the classroom could see nothing, and so they said the paper was empty. Which is the result we would all have expected. But the boys in the middle were the ones to provide the surprise: they each of them reported that they saw a series of lines on the paper!

The explanation is a psychological one. One of the basic drives behind humanity, behind the rise of our civilization, is an almost paranoiac desire to create order out of chaos. Instinctively we despise and fear chaos; we want to believe that we live in an ordered and reasonable universe. It's this desire, this fear, that gave rise to all our religions, and to our science as well. And so when the boys up front saw clearly nothing but dots on

the paper, they reported that. But the boys that sat a little further away couldn't see clearly what was there and so their minds
unconsciously connected the dots, formed an orderly array of
lines out of them.

And this, Maunder claimed, is what Percival Lowell's mind
had done when he looked at Mars. There were no canals, there
were only random markings on the planet, mountains perhaps,
or cracks in the surface; geological features only, scattered at
random over the surface, organized into canals only in the
mind of the man looking at them.

It was a convincing argument. It became even more convincing when, by 1947, astronomers like Gerald Kuiper, a Dutch-
man working in the United States, was able to report that the
planet was totally dry; he couldn't find any trace of water vapor
in the air, and there was virtually no oxygen there either. By
this time further heat measurements had shown that some
places on Mars did get warmer than freezing under the noonday
sun, but this didn't matter anymore: if the planet was without
water and without oxygen, it didn't matter if it occasionally
warmed up a bit.

The idea of life on Mars remained, but only in the comic
strips and in our poetic imaginings.

PART II

LIFE

My suspicion is not only that the universe is queerer than we suppose, but queerer than we can *suppose.*

—J.B.S. HALDANE

PART II

LIFE

My suspicion is not only that the universe is queerer than we suppose, but queerer than we can suppose.

—J.B.S. HALDANE

CHAPTER 4

Why?

IN 1975, the United States sent two spaceships, Viking I and Viking II, off on a year-long flight to Mars, at a cost of more than one *billion* dollars. The primary reason for the trip was to search the planet for signs of life.

Why?

Well, that's two questions, isn't it? The easy one is: "Why bother to look for life elsewhere in the universe?" That's easy because the answer is so obvious. The question of whether or not we are alone in the universe has to be the most important question we have ever asked. Is Earth the one and only spot in the entire universe where this unique condition of existence which we call *life* is to be found? Or is the universe full of life, in forms perhaps drastically different from our own? Are there people out there, or *beings* of some sort, with whom we could communicate? If you're not interested in this question, you're not intelligent enough to be reading this book; put it down and go turn on the television set.

The second question is tougher. Why *Mars?* Of all places in the universe, why should we expect life to exist there? When we sent rockets to the moon or to Venus, or flying by Jupiter and Saturn, or passing through the asteroid belt or the tail of a

23

comet, we didn't seriously look for life there. We knew we wouldn't find it. But the most pressing reason for spending one billion dollars of your tax money (or your father's or mother's) in a voyage to Mars was to look for life: because it very well might be there.

Why there? Why Mars? Partly, it must be admitted, because of John Carter and Buck Rogers and Flash Gordon; we were brought up, this generation that built the first interplanetary rockets, believing or imagining that Mars was teeming with all sorts of wonderful four-armed green-skinned white-furred creatures. We didn't *really* believe all that, of course, but just as an early childhood belief in Santa Claus lingers on in a subliminal sense as a vague feeling that in *some* way goodness must exist *somewhere* (even if it doesn't wear a red suit), so these stories have left behind in our imaginations a nagging suspicion that in *some* form, maybe semibacterial or microbial, in some form there just *ought* to be life up there on that lovely red planet.

But more importantly, there were good scientific reasons for suspecting the presence of life there. First of all, consider the planet and its resemblance to Earth.

Life on earth is made possible by the energy we get from the sun. We'll talk more about that later, but surely it's obvious that without the sun we'd be just a cold, dark speck of stony matter whirling alone through the universe, with temperatures so low that nothing could possibly live anywhere on this planet. In fact, for life to exist, the temperature on the surface of a planet must lie within a very narrow range of values: roughly between 0° and 100° centigrade.

How do we know this? Simply by observation. If you want to sterilize something, you can do it by putting it in boiling water. When you sterilize it, what you are doing is killing the germs, and we have found out over the centuries that we can kill germs by boiling the object in water. Now there's nothing magical about boiling water, it's just that water boils at a constant temperature—a temperature of 100° centigrade; and that temperature turns out to be hot enough to kill just about anything that lives, including most germs. (This is not an *absolute* criterion: some things can survive such temperatures, but practically everything dies if subjected to temperatures this high.) And we also know that things die when the temperature drops very low: when we have explored regions on earth where the temperature is maintained below 0° centigrade, such as the cold valleys of Antarctica or the high mountains of the Himalayas, we find nothing growing there, nothing living there (except perhaps a very few microbial forms of life).

Since on earth the temperatures in most regions don't vary by more than ten or twenty degrees centigrade during the whole year, from the depths of winter to the peaks of summer, this range of zero to a hundred might seem like a very large range to you. But the total variation of temperatures in the universe is much, much greater than this. The temperature of empty space is about *minus* 270°, while the temperature on the surface of the sun is about *plus* 5000°, and inside the sun or other stars it can reach temperatures of *millions* of degrees! In none of these places could life exist: it's too cold out in space, too hot on or inside stars. Life is suited, because of its dependence on a limited span of temperatures, for only a very few locations in the universe.

Why is life restricted to this small range of temperature? Primarily because of the behavior of water. In order for life to exist, as we'll see in more detail later, a very complex series of chemical reactions must take place easily and efficiently. In order for this to happen, the chemicals must be easily moved around so that they can contact each other. This means they must be dissolved in something, and water turns out to be the best possible solvent: it can dissolve more different types of chemicals more easily than anything else can. So the first requirement for life is the presence of water. And of course in order for chemicals to dissolve in it, the water must be in a liquid form. Since water freezes into solid ice at 0° and boils away into gaseous steam at 100°, we can only have liquid water between these two temperatures; and therefore life itself is restricted to this temperature interval. (Actually, the boiling and freezing points of water depend on how much of an atmosphere is present, so these temperatures may be different on different planets. But for any planet where other conditions are suitable for life, these temperatures won't change by *too* much, and the principle remains the same: we can have life only in the limited temperature range where liquid water may exist.)

So if we're going to look for life elsewhere, it has to be somewhere where the temperatures aren't too different from those on earth. Since the temperature on earth is controlled by the sun, and since the closer we get to the sun the hotter we'll be and the further away the colder, this means looking for a planet not much closer to the sun than the earth, and not much farther away.

Mercury, the planet closest to the sun, is much too close. Its mean distance (the orbits of the planets are not quite perfect circles, so they're not always at exactly the same distance from the sun; we'll talk about their mean or average distances) is less than 60 million kilometers. The earth's mean distance is about 150 million kilometers. This puts Mercury so close to the sun that its temperature during the daytime is 350°—much too high for life to exist. Even worse, it has no atmosphere, and since it's the atmosphere that spreads the warmth around a planet, this means that during the night its temperature drops to −170°: much too *cold* for life. So nobody is going to spend a billion bucks to look for life on Mercury.

The planet Venus is about 110 million kilometers from the sun; pretty close to the earth's distance. But it has a thick atmosphere of carbon dioxide, and this particular gas does a rather weird thing: it allows the sun's rays to penetrate right through, bringing their heat to the surface of the planet, but when the surface warms up and begins to radiate away its heat, the carbon dioxide traps it. The result is that heat comes in from the sun, and none of it (or only a little bit of it) escapes. Ever. And so the planet gets hotter and hotter. After all this time, Venus is at a temperature of about 480°, day and night. It's reached equilibirium at this point, it won't get any hotter, but that's plenty hot enough. Too hot for people, too hot for plants, too hot for bacteria or protozoa or even tourists. Furthermore, aside from the carbon dioxide the atmosphere of Venus is full of things like hydrochloric acid and sulfuric acid, which means it's even harder to breathe there than in the middle of a traffic jam on the New Jersey Turnpike on a summer day. So forget about anything living on Venus.

The next planet, third from the sun, is Earth. And, as Goldilocks said, "It's *ju-u-ust* right!" It's a very pleasant planet on which to live, at least until we start another world war and unleash all our stored hordes of nerve gases and biological killer bugs and cover the surface of the planet with radioactive waste.

The moon, of course, is just about the same distance from the sun as we are; its distance from earth is only a few thousand kilometers. But the moon has no atmosphere, and so the sun's rays beat down and heat the surface up to over a hundred degrees during the day, and then it cools right down to −153° at night: too hot for liquid water during the day, too cold for it at night; so no little moon-men running around.

The next planet, the fourth, is Mars. It's quite a bit farther away from the sun, nearly 230 million kilometers, and so it's a lot colder. Its mean temperature is −23°. Now this is below the freezing point of water, but this is the *mean* temperature. Because Mars has an atmosphere, the temperature variations won't be so striking as on the moon or Mercury, and it's possible that some slight variations would put some places on Mars at temperatures above zero: water might exist.

In fact, before we sent the Viking spacecraft we sent another series of interplanetary vessels out that way; these were the Mariner missions. They didn't land on Mars, but they flew close by and took pictures. Coming much closer to Mars than our telescopes on earth, they sent us back (via television) the clearest pictures we had ever had of the surface of the planet. As the pictures came back they were examined by a team of scientists with increasing excitement. Remember what we said in the last chapter about the Martian canals? If they existed, the Mariner pictures should show them in much better detail than they had ever been seen from earth.

They didn't. As the Mariner spacecraft came closer and closer to the planet and the pictures became clearer and clearer, we searched in vain for anything that looked remotely like a canal. They just simply weren't there. This was the first great disappointment for those who were hoping to find signs of a great civilization on Mars: the canals that had been seen by Lowell and Schiaperelli did not exist, they were figments of the imagination or designs drawn in the eye of the beholder, just as Maunder's schoolchildren had seen lines when they were shown nothing but a system of random dots.

But the Mariner pictures showed something nearly as good to those who were hoping just to find *any* form of life on Mars. They showed water! Well, not exactly water. The *maria* of Mars were not composed of seas any more than were the lunar *maria:* instead they are regions of darker rock than their surroundings, but solid rock just the same. But take a look at this photograph; the zig-zaggy channels shown here look exactly like a river! There's no water there now, but how else could such a

This photograph of channels cut through the Martian surface by flood or river waters was actually taken by a camera on board Viking as it was in orbit around Mars. JPL/NASA

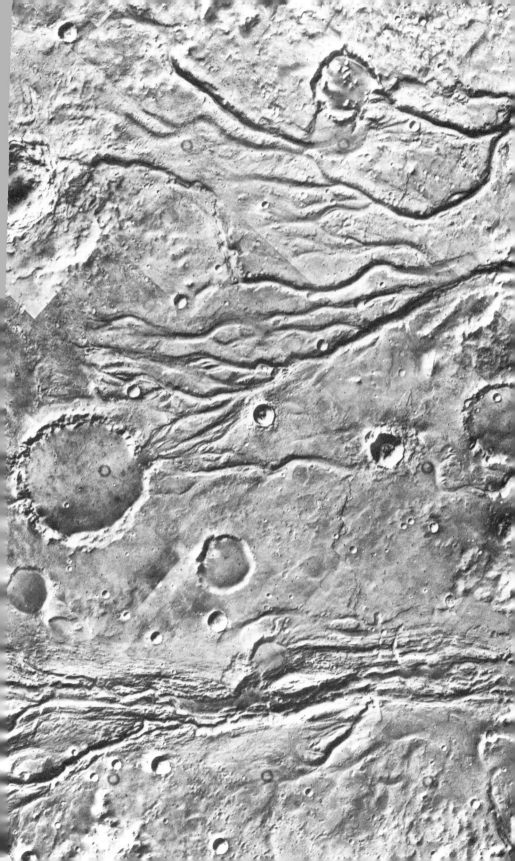

pattern be cut in the surface rock? Overwhelmingly the scientists studying this picture came to the conclusion that they were looking at the dry bed of an ancient river. Whether it had existed for a long time or whether it had been carved out by a gigantic flood, no one is certain. But certainly there has been water on Mars at some time. And where there is water there can be life!

The planets farther out than Mars—Jupiter, Saturn, Uranus, Neptune and Pluto—are too far away from the sun, too cold, to kindle thoughts of life in most scientists' minds. Possibly out there conditions might be right, but as you get farther and farther away from the sun it gets tougher and tougher to keep anything warm enough for anything to live.

Overwhelmingly, then, the conclusion has to be that if life can exist anywhere else in the solar system, besides on earth, Mars is the place to look.

But wait a minute. Let's say that Mars might be warm enough, okay, and it might have water on it (or did at some time), even if that's true—so what? Why should life come into being any place that's warm enough and wet enough?

If you take a bowl of warm water and let it sit for a few days or weeks, will life form in it? Out of nothing but water and warmth? Try it and see, but don't be surprised if your mother starts screaming at you when her best china bowl becomes full of slimy mold.

It turns out that your experiment is right and wrong. The slimy mold that eventually forms on the surface of the water is alive, all right, but it didn't arise just out of the water and the warmth. The warm water simply provided a nice new home for airborne bacteria to settle in and start a new community—to them the slimy mold isn't yucky, it's *family*.

The next step is to do the experiment more carefully: seal off the bowl of water from all air, keep it isolated from any possible invasion by bacteria, and see if life will form there spontaneously. In the nineteenth century, people thought that life *did* form spontaneously. They weren't so careful about garbage disposal and sanitation in those days, and the roads were often strewn with dead animals of one sort and another. It was a common observation that the flesh of such dead animals began to crawl with maggots after a few days. Where did the maggots come from? They weren't there when the animal was alive, and they weren't there when it died; but within a few days they appeared. The conclusion was that they were generated out of the nonliving tissue: this was called the *spontaneous generation* of life.

It wasn't until Louis Pasteur demonstrated that if the dead animals were kept isolated from the air no maggots would appear that this theory of the generation of life from nonliving materials was disproved. Today, on earth, the only way for a living thing to appear is for it to be born in some way from another living thing. But if we know this to be true, then how could we expect life to originate by itself on some other planet?

Hey, hold on a minute! If this is true, how did life originate on *this* planet? How did *we* get here?

CHAPTER 5

How?

IT'S A good question. Both the method of finding the answer and the answer itself lie in the concept of *evolution*.

If we want to find the roots from which we have grown, the most intelligent way to start is by investigating our history. Unfortunately that approach doesn't take us very far. We can trace our history fairly easily for the last few hundred years, but then we run into the Dark Ages when Europe dropped into anarchy and superstition, and we don't know very much about what was going on then. Few realistic records were kept as civilization dropped to a low ebb. Going back further, we pick up a little; we know a pretty fair amount about the Greek and Roman times, but then again as we pass into the further reaches of history, greater than a couple of thousand years, information becomes sparse again. History itself peters out into mythology when we go back five thousand years or so, and before that very little is known at all. We uncover ancient cities and find broken bits of pottery from which we try to trace out migration and trading routes, we find animal drawings on the walls of caves and try to understand how people hunted and farmed, and as we go further back in time we find we know nothing at all about our origins. We don't even know when men first came to America or what they found when they came, we don't know how people got to Australia or Alaska or where they came from or when they got there. We know nothing at all about history ten thousand years ago.

And ten thousand years is nothing, when we want to go back to the beginning. The earth is 4.5 billion years old. Life, as we'll soon discuss, began shortly after the earth formed. If we exaggerate our knowledge of history and say that we understand the past ten thousand years, we'd still only know about less than one-thousandth of one percent of the time since life first formed here on earth.

Obviously history can't take us far enough back in time to learn about the formation of life. We need another technique. Luckily we have one, due to evolution.

Let's talk about seashells. (No, I'm not changing the topic; seashells are the clue.) If you walk along the beach you can find a wonderful assortment of shells of many different kinds and shapes and colors. These shells are the skeletons of creatures who once were alive. Their skeletons are different from ours, they're worn on the outside of the creatures' bodies, and so they're called *exoskeletons*. It's easy enough to visualize how the two halves of a shell fit together to provide a space in which a little slimy creature can live and grow and flourish, protected from its enemies.

Well, we could get off into all kinds of interesting discussions about the nearly infinite variety of such creatures and all the different shells they grow, but we want to go into just one particular discussion: what would you find if you went for a walk on the same beach a couple of million years ago?

You'd find shells, lovely shells, similar to the ones you find today—but different. Similar, but different. And that's the clue.

The shells you find today are the nonliving remains of creatures that were once alive; any such remains are called *fossils*. Studying these shells, a biologist can tell what kinds of creatures are living in the oceans today.

The shells you would find washed up on the beach a few million years ago would be different, and biologists studying them could tell what kind of creatures lived in the oceans *then*. How do I know they would be different? Because we have found them. They're still around today, but they're hidden.

Imagine carrying out the following experiment: you go sailing off into the middle of the ocean. On your ship you carry a long, hollow cylinder—a few inches wide and hundreds of feet long. You tie a string to one end and drop it overboard, weighted on one end so that it falls upright to the bottom of the ocean. When it hits the bottom it will penetrate through the soft sand and sediment there, and the sediment will be pushed up into the cylinder. Then you yank on the string and bring it back up to the ship. If you're lucky, you'll find it still full of sediment.

Now the experiment really begins. When you examine this sample of the sea floor, called a *core*, you'll find it full of shells of all shapes and sizes. The sea floor, it turns out, is covered by thousands-of-feet-thick sediments composed largely of shells—the fossils of creatures that once lived in the ocean waters. How did these fossils come to cover the ocean floor? Simple, really. The creatures swim and float throughout the waters, but when they die their shells and skeletons just drop to the bottom. And they accumulate there, they build up into these sediments thousands of feet thick, over periods of millions and hundreds of millions of years! So when you look at your core, you find that the fossils at the top are composed of the shells of creatures identical to those still living today in the oceans, just as in the case of the shells we find when walking along the beach today.

But the shells at the bottom of the core are shells deposited many millions of years ago—and the fascinating fact is that these shells are different! Similar to the shells of creatures living today, but distinctly different. And so it is clear that creatures that lived millions of years ago were different from those living today.

This change in life forms, occurring more or less gradually throughout tremendous periods of time, is the process we call evolution. We'll talk later about how it takes place; what's important in this chapter is, first, the fact that is demonstrated by the different fossils that it *does* take place; and second, that it tells us a lot about how life formed and developed.

Because when we go back through the past eons of time by studying the fossils, we find that evolution in general has progressed from the simple to the complex. It's a tremendously complicated story, and what I'm saying here is just a quick and hasty simplification (you'll have to read whole books just about evolution if you really want to understand it, and you should), but the story shows an overall pattern of developing creatures that increased in complexity as time went by. That means that as we go back in time we find simpler and simpler creatures.

How far back in time can we go? Well, history took us back a few thousand years. The fossils found in the deep sea sediments can take us back more than a hundred million years. This is a tremendous advance over history, but it's still not nearly enough because a few hundred million years ago the life forms on earth were still tremendously complicated; obviously we haven't gone anywhere close to the beginning yet. And unfortunately that's as far as the ocean sediments can take us, because the floor of the ocean is continuously being swept under the rocks of the continents and there melted, destroyed, and recirculated throughout the earth—so the fossil story they carry is wiped out and lost.

Well, that's the bad news; the good news is that we can find other fossils on the continents, and these go back much further in time. We don't have such a nice, steady deposition of fossils on land as we do on the ocean floors, and so the fossil record is not quite as easy to read. There are large gaps in it, but little by little we have pushed the story back to nearly four billion years ago. At that time we didn't have any living creatures complex enough to have skeletons, and so no shells this old are found. In fact, the only way fossils this old can be preserved is if the living creature itself was trapped in a *sedimentary rock*. This is a rock that formed, not by eruption from a volcano, but slowly as little particles of sediment settled together and gradually were compressed into hard rock. A mineral called *chert* is responsible for trapping most of the really ancient fossils. Chert is useful because it precipitates quickly out of seawater, rapidly forming thin beds or little nodules of hard rock, trapping and preserving simple living things such as bacteria—which are very simple organisms and were among the first types of life to form.

In the deserts of western Australia, billions of years ago, there was water. Three and a half billion years ago a chert formation known today as the Warrawoona Group was forming, and as it formed it trapped several specimens of the life that was then prevalent on the surface of the earth. These consist of simple bacteria; you can see what they look like on the next page.

As you can see from the picture—which is one of the best we have—these bacteria fossils are not as clear to study or to understand as the pretty shells you can find on the beach. But they tell us a lot. They tell us that life didn't begin a few thousand years ago when our own history began. Instead, life began almost as long ago as the beginning of the earth itself. And they tell us that life began as very simple *organisms* (the name we give to any living thing: you, me, cockroaches, bacteria; we're all organisms). From the first simple organisms, life evolved into the marvelously complex spectra of complicated, sometimes weird organisms that fill the earth today—mosquitos, elephants, grass and flowers, fish and birds, people and football players.

Now again we're trailing off into different questions: the question of how life evolved into all these creatures is a fascinating one, but not the one we're interested in. That's the trouble with all of science: almost anything we begin to discuss leads to a variety of great questions we could talk about forever. But we have to stick to the point or we'll wander around and never reach any conclusions. The question we want to deal with here is how the first forms of life came into being, and why they might have done the same thing on Mars.

So how did these first simple life forms evolve out of nonliving things? Or did they? Was life created instead with a flash of light and a burst of cachinnation (look it up)?

Well, first of all, we have to decide what we mean by *life*. In just what way are living things different from nonliving things? And that is not an easy thing to decide.

The earliest fossils found on earth: bacterialike forms three and a half billion years old. J.W. SCHOPF, UCLA

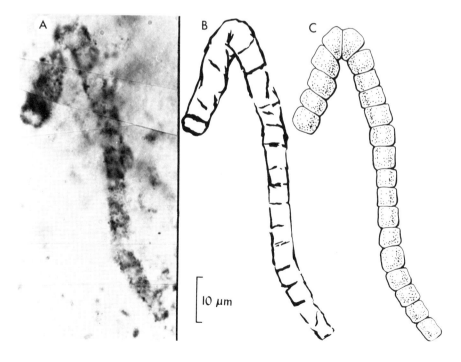

CHAPTER 6

Decisions,
Decisions. . .

AT FIRST GLANCE it looks easy. But at first glance *everything* looks easy: hitting curve balls and dunking basketballs, getting up on point in ballet slippers and playing a Bach sonata, drinking beer and kissing, all that stuff looks easy—until you try it. Let's look at the problem a little more closely.

All right, living things are different from nonliving things, so it should be easy to state clearly and distinctly the differences and in doing so we can define what we mean by life.

So go ahead. Try.

Right, then. What's the difference between you and a stone? Easy. You move, the stone doesn't. So first of all, there is motion.

But there isn't, is there? Because a blade of grass can't move, neither can a flower or a tomato—and all these things are alive.

Okay then, you breathe and the stone doesn't. But again, neither does the grass or the flower or the—well, you get the idea.

Not as easy as it looked at first glance, is it? We have to find some criterion that applies to *everything* that is alive and to *nothing* that is not alive.

Animals eat and breathe and defecate and mate, but plants

don't; they photosynthesize and pollinate. Animals kill other animals; plants sway in the wind and let their fellow plants co-exist. Animals move from place to place, plants are content where they are. (You have to begin to wonder what's so great about us animals, don't you?)

Anyhow, it's clear that different forms of living things do different things. What is it that *all* life does?

Well, we grow, don't we? We take in food and energy from our environment and we use it to build ourselves, to get bigger. We eat our broccoli (well, some of us do) and our steak, and we digest it and turn it into muscle and bone; plants absorb water and nutrients from the ground and use the energy of sunlight to turn it into a longer stem, a lovelier flower. We do it in different ways, but all living things do it.

But so do some nonliving things. A fire, for instance. If you take a match and set your house on fire, what happens? I mean, aside from when your parents find out. Consider the flame of the match. It is born when you strike the match, a pretty little red and blue flame. As it feeds upon the curtains it gets bigger and hotter, as it consumes the furniture and the wooden floors and walls it grows and gets bigger and stronger. And finally when the firemen come it dies.

Is the flame alive?

No.

But what is the difference between it and living things?

Let's try once more. Living things reproduce themselves, they have babies. Stones can't do that.

But fire can.

Suppose you hold a flaming match in your hand. There's just the one fire. But then you touch it to a piece of paper and lo and behold: another little flame appears. The fire has reproduced itself. And it doesn't need you to help it, fires do it every day by themselves—think of forest fires.

And fires aren't the only nonliving things that can grow and reproduce themselves. If you drop a grain of salt into a concentrated salt solution, molecules of salt from the solution will crystallize out on that first grain: the grain will grow. And the disturbance it induces in the solution will under some conditions influence other molecules to precipitate out and form other crystals just like the original grain: the first grain is now a daddy!

You can think of all sorts of processes or criteria to differentiate living from nonliving things, but I'll bet you get them all wrong. It's a very tough question. In fact, several years ago when a conference on the origin of life was held by the National Aeronautic and Space Administration (NASA), the best biologists in the world found that they were arguing for days about this very question. In the end they decided that there was only one hard and fast rule: living things not only reproduce themselves, they *evolve*. And that is the one thing that all living things can do and that *no* nonliving things can do.

Evolution turns out to be the criterion for life. And so there's no getting away from it: in order to understand how life originated on Earth and how or why it might originate on Mars, we must understand how evolution works. To do this we'll get into the nitty-gritty of life itself, and this can be done on two different levels: the biological and the chemical.

First, biology. What do *all* living things look like, when you look very, very closely?

CHAPTER 7

The Living Cell

THEY LOOK like this:

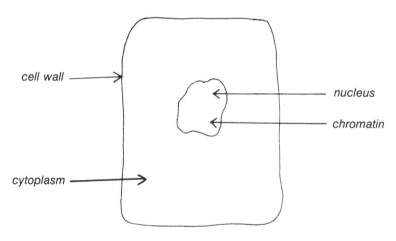

This is a *cell*. Not the kind you keep prisoners in, but the kind you keep life in. The most important part of it, just as in the case of the jail cell, is the wall around it, the *cell wall*, the thing that separates each individual cell from the rest of the universe. ·

Because this was the beginning of life. Somehow, somewhere

on the primitive earth, the first cell wall formed and isolated the stuff inside it from the stuff outside it; and inside this first cell life truly began.

There are differences among cells. For example, the first living things to form had cells without a nucleus. But all living things are composed of some sort of cells, not too different from this one. The simplest creatures are composed of just one cell (things like bacteria or algae) and the more complex are composed of unbelievable numbers of cells. (There are more cells in your body than there are stars in the galaxy or grains of sand on the beach.)

This means, of course, that each cell is tiny. In fact, they can be seen only under a good microscope. Their sizes vary, but roughly they are only a few microns large. A micron is about a ten-thousandth of an inch (exactly one ten-thousandth of a centimeter).

If you look at the cell of any living thing, you would immediately recognize it for what it is. (Well, *I* would; I'm not sure how bright you are.) The point is that *all* living organisms are made of these very similar building parts. All cells are formed according to the same laws, they all grow in a similar way. And that's *all* cells, whether they are part of a carrot or a finger or an oak tree or a snake's gizzard. It makes you think that maybe all forms of life evolved from the same ancestor, doesn't it? Because if life had formed in different ways at different times, wouldn't the descendants of these different parents look totally different? This is a serious question in regard to the origin of life, and while the answer isn't totally sure, it certainly looks from this evidence that we are all descended from the same type of thing. We'll see later on some other evidence on this point.

Well, let's get back to this cell. It's only a few thousandths of an inch big, but it's pretty complicated and well organized. Inside the cell wall, separated from everything else outside it, is a sticky liquid (mostly water) called the *cytoplasm*. And inside this, enclosed by a semipermeable membrane (that is, a wall that allows some things to transfer back and forth through it) is the *nucleus*. Inside the nucleus is some clumpy material called *chromatin*, which will become very important.

The basic process of life is the continued production of new cells. This is necessary, first of all, for the organism to grow, and second of all because all cells must die. If no new cells are grown, then the entire organism must die.

Well, okay, the entire organism must die someday, that's true, but as for me I'm not quite ready yet. Are you? You see, every day many of our cells die and are replaced by newly born cells that take over their function and keep us—the organism—alive. Eventually we will stop producing new cells, and as our old cells die we reach a point where there aren't enough of them around and working to keep us alive, and then we have to die. The question of why we stop producing new cells is another one of those questions that would take us away from this book and into another, so we won't ask it. (Actually, if I knew, I'd tell you. Nobody knows why death has to occur. Maybe some scientist in your generation will find the answer. Maybe *you* will.)

Anyway, back to life! What is happening in our bodies as we live is that a whole bunch of different kinds of cells (all basically similar, of course) are doing a whole bunch of different kinds of jobs. Some are taking in oxygen, some are forming blood, some are forming urine, some are thinking, some are digesting lunch, some are looking, some are listening, some are tasting. Each of these thousands of millions of cells in your body are basically similar to each other but slightly different—because they each have their own particular job to do. When a new cell is formed, it also has to do its own job. It wouldn't do, for example, if a stomach cell were to form in your lungs, or if a vision cell were to form in your intestine—and this doesn't happen. When a new cell forms, it is a perfect duplicate of its parent cell and so it is perfectly suited to do the same job. How do we get such perfection?

In simple cells without a nucleus, such as the cell of a bacteria, the cell simply splits in two. Each new cell is just half the old, identical to it but smaller. It grows to the same size, then splits apart and we have four cells from the original one, and each is identical. This process is called *fission*.

In the more complicated nucleated cells of which we are composed, such a simple process wouldn't work. All of the nucleus, for example, might be in one half and not in the other. The two new cells would then not be perfect duplicates of the old. We have a different process, called *mitosis*.

In mitosis the chromatin within the nucleus becomes organized into a number of threads which we call *chromosomes*. The chromosomes then form into two groups that are identical to each other, and that move away to opposite sides of the nucleus. The nucleus then splits in two, each new nucleus moves to opposite ends of the cell, and then the cell splits in two—and the two new cells formed are identical to each other and to the original cell.

From this description you can see that the chromosomes hold the key to the duplication of the old cell. These chromosomes are divided into thousands of sections called *genes*. It is the number and arrangements of these genes that characterize the cell. Think of the genes as words, and the chromosomes as sentences, and the cell as a book. The way you arrange the words into sentences decides how good a book you will have, and what kind of a book you will have—a great one like this book, or a lousy one like . . . well, you know.

In this manner, then, the original cell is duplicated. But only if the process works perfectly. What happens if one gene is incorrectly placed, or changed in some way, when the chromatin forms into chromosomes and the cell splits? The new cell formed from this deranged gene will be different—slightly or greatly different depending on how the gene was changed or rearranged. This different cell is called a *mutant*. The mutant cell, when it duplicates itself, will do just that—it will produce a new mutant, rather than another cell like the original one from which it itself grew. In this way, the mutation can spread throughout the organism. If the mutation is a defective one, the new cells will not be able to do their job: what we are doing here is growing a cancer. Mutant lung cells that cannot breathe properly, for example, might spread and take over a lung, and then the organism cannot breathe and it will choke to death. So don't smoke, because cigarette smoke *can* produce mutations in your lung cells.

Some of our cells are called *reproductive* cells: their job is to reproduce the entire organism. When you were born, for example, an egg cell from your mother combined with a sperm cell from your father and began the process of forming *you*. How did this new creature being formed in your mother's womb know that it was to be a human being rather than an ape or a blade of grass?

By this same process, simply raised to a more complex level. The genes in the reproductive cells carry the information that describes the parent, so that when the male and female reproductive cells combine, the creature formed is not only a person but a combination of the two individuals who got together to form him (her, it).

And when a mutation occurs in the reproductive cells, the entire newly formed organism is a mutant.

Yuck.

But not always. I mean, not always *yuck*. Mutations are simply creatures that are *different*, not necessarily inferior. It's true that living organisms are so highly organized that any random mutation is likely to produce a change that is for the worse, but this is not necessarily true. Sometimes the mutant might be superior. The mutation is not necessarily a major event—perhaps the mutant looks just like everyone else but is a fraction of an inch taller, or stronger, or has better eyesight or a better brain.

The point I'm leading up to, of course, is evolution. Because the mutant creature will reproduce the mutation, and if the mutation has led to a slightly superior and different creature, then that creature may produce others and so on, taking over and dominating the original species—and what we have done is evolve a new creature.

This is all not necessarily true in each case—the new mutation may be inferior (most of the time it will be)—and whether it is or not it could eventually die out. But *sometimes* a new creature will evolve. And so we have birds evolving from snakes, snakes from amphibians, amphibians from fish . . . and somewhere along the line, nearly four billion years after it all started, you and I came along.

But before we did—billions of years before we came along—the first life form organized itself into existence, the first living organism in a nonliving world evolved. How on earth—literally—did this happen?

In order to understand this, we have to go back to the basic building blocks of nature: the different atoms of which the entire universe—living and nonliving—is composed. The study of the behavior of the elements (or atoms) is called *chemistry*, and later on in this book when we talk about the experiments on Mars we shall see how important this fact is: that all living processes, all biology, is actually chemistry.

You hear a lot of nonsense these days in television commercials and in conversation about how we shouldn't want any chemicals in our foods, we shouldn't put chemicals into our bodies, our food and bodies should remain *pure*. All this talk is the purest nonsense because all of our food and all of our bodies is composed of nothing but chemicals! And some of these chemicals can be bad for us, of course, but others are not; and some are absolutely necessary. The important thing is the nature of the chemicals, not the fact that they are chemicals rather than "natural products." Nothing is more "natural" than tobacco with all its associated tars and crud, and nothing is more harmful to you. On the other hand, it makes no difference if a water supply is carbonated "naturally" in the soils of France or "chemically" in a factory in Trenton—it's still nothing but a solution of CO_2 and H_2O and not particularly healthy or unhealthy either way.

The point of all this is that we ourselves, and all forms of life, eat and breathe and digest nothing but chemicals. All life, every living thing, is composed of chemicals reacting with each other in purely chemical systems.

And so in order to understand life, we must understand the chemistry behind it.

Sorry about that.

CHAPTER 8

Chemistry (and How to Love It)

THE ENTIRE universe in all its complexity and uniqueness is composed of only ninety-two different kinds of atoms, arranged in a nearly infinite number of ways. The thing that makes one kind of atom behave differently from another is its *electronic structure*: the number and arrangement of its electrons. Each atom looks roughly like a miniature solar system, with the electrons taking the place of the planets and whirling around a central nucleus:

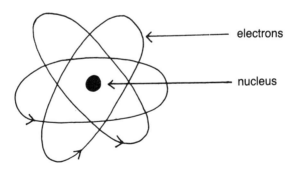

The simplest atom, hydrogen, has just one electron; the heaviest atom that occurs naturally on earth, uranium, has ninety-two. We have made atoms in the laboratory with more than one hundred electrons, but the atoms that are necessary for life are among the simplest and have just a very few electrons.

For a full, healthful, and happy life, with all of your physical and mental processes whipping along at top speed, you need an abundance of practically every element that exists. So you have to eat carrots and broccoli and lettuce and all sorts of awful stuff. But for life simply to exist, without worrying about how healthy it is, we really need only five basic kinds of atoms (each kind of atom is called an *element*). These are shown in the table just below. (You will have to learn some day, so you might as well do it now, not to skip tables, although the temptation is great. Scientists like tables because they're an *easy* way to present data, not a hard way. So look at the table, okay?)

Table 1. The elements necessary for life.

Element	Chemical Symbol	Number of Electrons
Hydrogen	H	1
Carbon	C	6
Nitrogen	N	7
Oxygen	O	8
Phosphorus	P	15

It isn't necessary to know the actual number of electrons for each of these elements; I only put them there to emphasize the fact that the distinction between one element and another is based solely on the number of electrons each has. So every atom of hydrogen has one electron, every atom of carbon has six, etc.

Since each of these is necessary for life to form, it's silly to say that any one of them is more important than any other—but carbon is the most important. What I mean is, suppose you have a football team with nine good men and one guy like Herschel Walker or Doc Blanchard (ask your father) or Red Grange (you shouldn't have to ask), and one guy who can't do much of anything. They're all necessary for the team, even the guy who can't do anything but tie his shoelaces, because if you don't have eleven men out there on the field you have to forfeit the game. So they're *all* necessary. But surely Herschel Walker is *more* necessary—you might find someone else to substitute for the others, but you need your star.

In the chemistry of life, carbon is the star.

This is because carbon can share electrons and thus bond with up to four elements in very stable forms, and thus it can form a bewildering array of *molecules* (which are combinations of atoms). All atoms of any chemical interest can form these bonds, or similar ones—because all chemistry is composed of atoms forming molecules—but no other atom except carbon can form such large, complicated molecules. A typical biological molecule might look like this:

$$H - \underset{\underset{H}{|}}{\overset{\overset{H}{|}}{C}} - \underset{\underset{H}{|}}{\overset{\overset{H}{|}}{C}} - O - H \qquad (1)$$

or this:

$$K - C \equiv N \qquad (2)$$

or this:

$$H - N - \underset{\underset{H}{|}}{\overset{\overset{H}{|}}{C}} - \overset{\overset{O}{\|}}{C} - O - H \qquad (3)$$

Molecule 1 is a chemical that is absolutely vital to many forms of life, such as college students and drunk drivers: it is *ethyl alcohol*, and it is the stuff that makes you (hopefully not *you*) drunk. Its formula can be written in a kind of shorthand notation as C_2H_5OH. To show how important the precise number of atoms in a molecule is, if we take out one of the carbon groups we would end up with CH_3OH—and this is *methyl alcohol*, sometimes known as wood alcohol; it's the kind of alcohol you often get when people try to make their own alcohol, and it's a poison. It can make you drunk, but it can also blind you or kill you.

Molecule 2 is potassium cyanide, one of the deadliest poisons known to man (and woman; Agatha Christie used it often). And molecule 3 is a substance known as *glycine*, which is one of the most important chemicals for all living creatures; we'll hear more about it later.

In the chemical diagrams we have used the *symbols* for each element; this obviously makes it easier to write and to read. Each of the ninety-two elements has its own symbol, but we'll need only the five listed in Table 1. You'll also have noticed the lines between the symbols. Each line corresponds to a chemical bond holding the atoms together. A double bond, such as the one between carbon and oxygen in glycine, is stronger than a single bond; the triple bond in cyanide is even stronger. It is the ability to make these different bonds between different atoms that makes carbon so useful in forming complicated molecules.

And they do get complicated. In the nonliving world, most molecules consist of less than a dozen atoms. Water, for example, has three atoms in its molecule (H_2O); salt has two (NaCl, sodium and chlorine); air is composed mostly of molecules with two atoms of oxygen (O_2) or nitrogen (N_2); glass is mostly a three-atom molecule of silicon and oxygen (SiO_2); and a typical kind of rock material is the mineral felspar (potassium aluminum silicate—$KAlSi_3O_8$), with thirteen atoms per molecule.

These are typical of the complexity of the nonliving world around us: molecules with from two to about a dozen atoms in them. We hardly ever see any molecules with more than a few dozen atoms in them—except in the living world. Typical *organic* molecules, in living creatures, can have hundreds of *thousands* of atoms in them, linked together generally as a long chain of carbon atoms bonded to each other and to a few thousand more nitrogen, hydrogen, oxygen, and phosphorus atoms. The basis for all these organic compounds is the chain of carbons. For example, a typical *amino acid* (which is a basic molecule in the living process) might look like this:

$$\begin{array}{c}
\text{H} \quad \text{H} \quad \text{O} \quad \text{H} \quad \text{H} \quad \text{O} \quad \text{H} \quad \text{H} \quad \text{O} \quad \text{H} \quad \text{H} \quad \text{O} \\
| \quad\; | \quad\; \| \quad\; | \quad\; | \quad\; \| \quad\; | \quad\; | \quad\; \| \quad\; | \quad\; | \quad\; \| \\
\text{H} - \text{N} - \text{C} - \text{C} - \text{N} - \text{C} - \text{C} - \text{N} - \text{C} - \text{C} - \text{N} - \text{C} - \text{C} - \\
| \qquad\qquad | \qquad\qquad\quad | \qquad\qquad\quad | \\
\text{R}_1 \qquad\qquad \text{R}_2 \qquad\qquad \text{R}_3 \qquad\qquad \text{R}_4
\end{array}$$

$$\begin{array}{c}
\text{H} \quad \text{H} \quad \text{O} \\
| \quad\; | \quad\; \| \\
\ldots\ldots \text{N} - \text{C} - \text{C} - \text{O} - \text{H} \\
| \\
\text{R}_i
\end{array}$$

where each group R_1 to R_4 to R_i (where i can be any number up to the thousands) represents another long chain of carbon atoms stretching down from the main chain, and where the dots (. . . . .) represent the same types of atoms, too many to write down here.

So carbon, as we see, can form a chain of atoms linked into molecules many thousands of atoms long, and these molecules are more complex than any nonliving molecules. In fact, until the nineteenth century we had thought that organic chemistry is so much more complicated than *inorganic* chemistry (the chemistry of nonliving things) because it is a totally different ballgame—it was thought that life is somehow mysterious and different and not run according to the same rules of chemistry that govern the rest of the universe. It was thought, for example, that organic molecules can only be made by living creatures, by the life process. A mysterious "vital force" was thought to exist in all living things, and this "force" was a necessary component of any organic molecule.

Not so.

In 1828 a German chemist, Friedrich Wöhler, astounded the world of science by creating in his laboratory a flask of *urea*. Now urea is the chemical of which urine is basically composed, and every one of us creates copious quantities of that every time we go to the bathroom, so what was the big deal?

The big deal was the Wöhler created it not in the *lavatory* but in the *laboratory* (what a big difference a couple of letters make). He took a plain *inorganic* chemical, ammonium cyanate, and by a careful heating experiment he found that it was changed into urea, a real organic chemical produced in animal bodies. It looks like this:

$$
\begin{array}{ccc}
\text{H} & \text{O} & \text{H} \\
| & \| & | \\
\text{H}-\text{N}- & \text{C}- & \text{N}-\text{H}
\end{array}
$$

Ammonium cyanate is a simple molecule composed of the same atoms, C, N, H, and O; chemists had already known how to form it out of those atoms. So now for the first time a chemist could take these four kinds of atoms and form first ammonium cyanate and then urea—from simple atoms they could form an organic molecule, without adding any mysterious "vital force!" The chemistry of living things was shown to be no different from that of nonliving things.

Not different, but vastly more complicated. Just a few years later, when everyone and his brother and sister were producing one kind of organic molecule after another in the excitement of creating a new science, poor Friedrich Wöhler was so bewildered by the enormous complexity of this monster he had created that he wailed: "Organic chemistry drives me mad! It's like a primeval tropical forest full of the most remarkable stuff—a dreadful endless jungle into which you'd better not enter because there seems to be no way out!"

From that prosaic beginning, the synthesis of urea, has come all the wonders of modern organic chemistry—the production of pharmaceuticals, medicines, and vaccines, without which life was so much more painful and bitter to our parents and grandparents. And out of it also came the knowledge of the basic chemistry of life—and how it began.

CHAPTER 9

The Chemistry
of Life

WE CAN THINK of life as involving two processes, and both are based on the concept of death. The first process is simply the very nonsimple process of warding off death—of staying alive. This involves a multitude of different things for different organisms: for us it includes breathing and eating and watching out for speeding drivers and not smoking, for asparagus it involves photosynthesis and assimilation of water, for vampires it involves finding tender virgins and getting back to the casket before dawn. It means different things for different organisms, but basically it involves the work of life itself—the life of the individual organism.

The other process has to do with not allowing the death of the entire line of organisms which are similar to each other. Because the first process *must* end in failure—each of us must die eventually, you and me and the asparagus plant and even the vampire, God willing. But there is something in each of us which wants to create other creatures like ourselves, so that even when we die there will be something of us left alive in our children. This urge—no, it's more than merely an *urge*; it's a basic concomitant of every form of life—this *life process* is called reproduction, or replication. It is the process by which an organism produces another nearly identical organism.

The concept of *nearly identical* is very important. Most people want to have children. Note that I didn't say that most people want merely to *create life:* it's important that when you produce a baby it be a *human* baby. If your offspring were a cockroach or a flower or an antelope, it would be alive but the feeling just wouldn't be the same.

So the chemicals in your body have to do two things: they have to keep you alive, carry out the processes of breathing and digesting and secreting and excreting and all that; and they have to reproduce you in some way. It's the *chemicals* in your body that have to do this because there isn't anything else in there!

In order to carry out these two distinctly different processes, life on earth has evolved two distinctly different kinds of molecules. The molecules that carry on the everyday processes of keeping the organism alive are called *proteins.* Our bodies are made of proteins and run by proteins: they are the principal material of our skins, muscles, nerves, fat and blood. To understand them, let's start at the beginning.

All organic molecules are chains of carbon atoms, associated with the other four atoms O,N,H, and P. If you look back over some of the examples we gave before, you'll notice a grouping of atoms that looks like this:

$$\begin{array}{c} \text{O} \\ \| \\ -\ \text{C} - \text{O} - \text{H} \end{array}$$

This COOH grouping is called an acidic group, and any molecule that has it is an acid. (Inorganic acids like HCl do not need this group, but all organic acids have it). All proteins are formed by joining together a large number of organic acids. But they have to be a particular type of acid. Again, you'll notice

that some of our previous examples have a group that looks like
this:

This NH_2 grouping is called an *amino* group, and organic acids
that have it are called amino acids. A protein, then, is simply
a long chain of amino acids. And believe it or not, these proteins are what *you* are.

Now, a person as complicated as yourself must necessarily be
composed of a terrific number of different proteins. There are
thousands of different kinds of proteins in each one of us, and
each protein does a different job. And every different kind of
organism has different kinds of proteins in it to do these jobs
which keep the organism alive and kicking.

But all of the proteins in the living world have similarities.
It's amazing, but with all the *millions* of different forms of life
that exist today and have existed in the past on this earth of
ours, all the different proteins are formed from only about two
dozen different amino acids. The important ones are listed in
Table 2 (page 59).

The simplest amino acid out of which our proteins are made
is *glycine*. Remember its formula? It's NH_2CH_2COOH:

$$\begin{array}{ccccc} & H & & H & & O \\ & | & & | & & \| \\ H- & N & - & C & - & C & -O-H \\ & & & | \\ & & & H \end{array}$$

All of the amino acids found in proteins are very similar; each
one of those listed in Table 2 can be written in the same way

with only one change: the bottom H is changed to a complicated group of atoms:

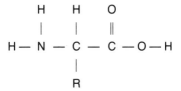

where the symbol R represents a side chain, which can be anything from a single H atom (in glycine) to a simple carbon
group like CH_3 (in alanine) to more complicated arrangements
of carbon and hydrogen and nitrogen in rings and circles and
bangles and beads, so to speak. Aside from this one difference,
all the amino acids that make up proteins are exactly the same.

But if the amino acids are so similar, and there are only
about two dozen of them, how can there be thousands of different proteins for each one of millions of different species (a
species is a *kind* or type of organism)?

Easy.

Just think about what you're doing now. You're reading a
page on which are different words. How many different words
are there in the language? For all practical purposes, an infinite
number. That is, we're not limited as to the number of words
in the language by any limitation of the structure of the language itself but only by the limits to our own memories. We
can make as many words as we like—and they're all made out
of only twenty-six letters: about the same number as the number
of different amino acids.

And think how we can make words totally different even with
the same letters, just rearranging them a little. Think what different meanings these two sentences have:

1. My god is dead.
2. My dog is dead.

Table 2. The amino acids of life.

Amino Acid	Abbreviation
Alanine	Ala
Arginine	Arg
Asparagine	AspN
Aspartic Acid	Asp
Cysteine	CysH
Cystine	CyS
Dibromotyrosine	—
Diiodotyrosine	—
Glutamic Acid	Glu
Glutamine	GluN
Glycine	Gly
Histidine	His
Hydroxylysine	Hylys
Hydroxyproline	Hypro
Isoleucine	Ileu
Leucine	Leu
Lysine	Lys
Methionine	Met
Phenylalanine	Phe
Proline	Pro
Serine	Ser
Threonine	Yhr
Thyroxine	—
Tryptophane	Tryp
Tyrosine	Tyr
Valine	Val

We can make words of totally different meaning by simply rearranging the letters, or by adding new ones—a *dog* is a totally different creature from a *doge*. (Look it up, that's what dictionaries are for.)

And it's the same way with amino acids and proteins. From the twenty-six different "letters" (amino acids) we can make thousands of millions of different "words" (proteins), and each word has a different meaning (does a different job in a different creature).

Now, one last thought before we leave the proteins. *Why* should all living creatures on earth be formed from just these few amino acids, all of which are so similar to each other? If life formed at different places and times, under different conditions, with no relationship to each other, and with a virtually infinite different number of totally different amino acids to choose from, why should they all end up with just these limited types?

Hey, that rings a bell, doesn't it? Remember we said that all living things are composed of quite similar structures called *cells?* It's beginning to look as if all life on earth is related to each other.

And here's something else: *the rotation of polarized light.*

Ordinary light is a combination of electric and magnetic waves, called *electromagnetic* waves. One of them, intersecting a screen, might look like this:

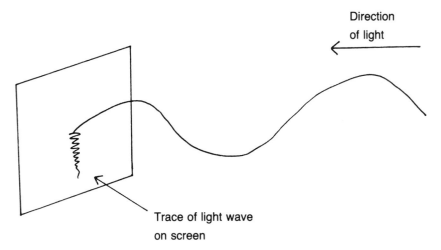

Direction
of light

Trace of light wave
on screen

If the screen were made of photographic film, and if the room were dark except for the one light wave, the *trace* of the wave on the film could be seen as a bright line. In reality, ordinary light is made up of many such waves, all rising and falling in different directions rather than just the single vertical wave shown above. The trace of these waves on the film would be a very large number of lines rotated at all angles around the one line we've been talking about:

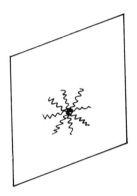

In fact, there would be so many lines that they would all merge together and the trace of ordinary light would be a circle. But it is possible to produce light in which *all* the waves are vertical, so that the trace of this light is a single line on the film. This is called *polarized* light. Now what has this to do with our amino acids?

Let's take a typical amino acid:

$$
\begin{array}{ccccccc}
\text{H} & & \text{H} & & \text{O} & & \\
| & & | & & \| & & \\
\text{H}-\text{N}- & & \text{C}- & & \text{C}-\text{O}-\text{H} & & \\
& & | & & & & \\
& & \text{X} & & & &
\end{array}
$$

where the symbol X stands for any possible grouping of further atoms, such as a long chain of carbon and oxygen and hydrogen atoms. Remember, this is really a picture of what the molecule actually looks like, with the chemical symbols used in place of pictures of the actual atoms. Now let's put a mirror next to it, and look at the *mirror image* of the molecule:

```
    H   H   O                    O   H   H
    |   |   ||                    ||  |   |
H—  N — C — C —O—H  |  H—O— C — C — N —H
    |                              |
    X                              X
```

These two molecules are chemically identical: NH_2C_2XHOOH (or $C_2NXO_2H_4$, if you prefer). But there is a *structural* difference between them, similar to the difference between a right-handed and a left-handed glove. The difference can be easily seen if you realize that, although I have written these molecules as if they are flat (I had to, because the paper is flat), actually the H and O atoms stick out at all different directions from the paper: the molecules are *curved.* Now consider your hands. Go on, look at them. If you hold them flat, with the fingers stiff, you can place one hand right up against the other. If the front and back of your hands were identical, then the two hands would now be identical. They fit together perfectly.

But now curve your fingers and try to do the same thing. There is no way you can make your hands lie next to each other so that the same part of each hand lies against its partner on the other hand: for example, the thumbnail and the first joint of the thumb, and the nails and first joints of all the other fingers. No matter how you twist and turn, even if you rip your hands right off at the wrists, you can't do it. Go ahead, try.

It's the same with these curved organic molecules. The two different forms are said to be *mirror images* just as your hands are mirror images of each other (look at them in the mirror).

They are also called *optical isomers*, because their effect on light is different, at least their effect on polarized light. If a beam of polarized light is shone through a solution of amino acids which is composed of only one of the two mirror images, the trace of the light on the screen will be rotated either right or left.

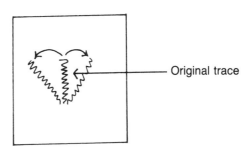

Original trace

One of the "gloves" rotates it to the right and is called the *dextrorotatory* form, the other rotates it to the left and is called the *levorotatory* form. Whenever we make amino acids in the laboratory, or whenever they are made by any nonliving process, such as in meteorites or out in space, equal mixtures of both forms are created. This is called a *racemic* mixture, and has no effect on polarized light because half the molecules rotate it to the right and half to the left. These two effects thus cancel out.

But in all amino acids formed in the living process on earth, only the *levorotatory* form is formed. Somehow life has a preference for this one structure. Now that's weird, isn't it? Why should it be so?

And why should all living cells be so similar?

And of all the millions of possible amino acids, why should all life be made of just the twenty-six of Table 2?

It begins to look as if all life is related; in fact, as if all life on earth has come from a common ancestor, from one primeval form that happened to begin with just the levorotatory form of these twenty-six amino acids which it built up into a living cell. Some scientists think, indeed, that all of us—all life on earth—is descended from one individual cell that gathered itself together out of the various organic chemicals it found billions of years ago on what was then a lifeless planet whirling around the sun.

CHAPTER 10

The Chemistry of Life (2: Nucleic Acids)

THERE'S one more type of organic molecule that has to be formed in order for life to evolve, and that's the type of molecule that takes charge of the second life process, the replication of cells and whole organisms. The basic question here is a fascinating and perplexing one that has only recently been answered: how does a unique cell (or a unique whole organism) duplicate itself instead of forming any one of the infinite varieties that might exist? How does a liver cell reproduce itself to form another liver cell rather than a lung cell or a blood cell? How does a mother rat produce a baby rat instead of a baby kangaroo?

The answer to this lies in the *genetic code.*

And the basis of the genetic code are the *nucleic acids,* the second distinct group of organic molecules that constitute what we call life. The proteins are the molecules that carry on the day-to-day living processes: they are the things that make us breathe, eat, walk, and think. The job of the nucleic acids is to create new proteins, and to create exactly the right ones. When they goof up—cancer and mutations! (More about that later.)

You remember what the cell looks like, of course. If you don't, go back to page 41. The cytoplasm, the great mass of the cell that does the work the cell has to do, is composed of protein molecules. But in the nucleus a different kind of organic molecule is formed. Because they are formed in the nucleus, and because they are acids, they are called the nucleic acids.

The nucleic acids are themselves built up of other complex organic molecules, just as the proteins are. In this case the simpler molecules are bases, sugars, and phosphoric acid, but rather than go into details of the chemistry—which are similar to the construction of proteins, as discussed in the last chapter—I think it will be more interesting to talk about the star of the show, deoxyribonucleic acid, or DNA for short.

There are many more than a trillion cells in your body, and more than 50 million molecules in every one of those cells. Out of all those molecules, the largest are those of DNA; one single DNA molecule can contain millions of individual atoms. What does this monster look like?

For many years nobody knew. We first became interested in the subject back in 1928, when an English scientist named Frederick Griffith found that he could change harmless bacteria into pneumonia-causing bacteria by injecting them with a chemical taken from other dead pneumonia-causing bacteria. Although nobody really wants to create germs that can kill people,* this experiment caused great excitement because it showed for the first time that inherited characteristics of a cell depend purely on chemicals. The hunt was on—to find *which* chemical.

It took another fifteen years of constant work before a group of American scientists at the Rockefeller Institute showed that only one chemical was always present in the characteristic-altering experiments. This was DNA.

And now the question was to understand the structure of DNA that would account for this nearly miraculous power. An-

---

*Wouldn't it be nice if this were really true?

other ten years of intense scientific collaboration and competition followed, until finally in 1953, an English group (which included an American working that year at Cambridge) proposed a structure that has since proven to be correct. The story of that research has been excitingly told in *The Double Helix*, by James Watson, who was the American working in that group.

Think of a ladder.

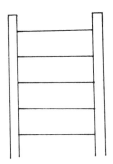

Now twist the ladder into a spiral staircase.

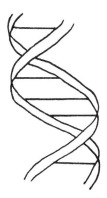

This is DNA. The curved vertical sides of the ladder are made of chains of sugars and phosphoric acids, and the rungs of the ladder are called bases. The trick of reproduction is based on the bases.

There are two things a DNA molecule has to do, remember. First, it has to be a unique thing in itself. That is, it has to be the DNA of a human skin cell, or a rat blood cell, or an elephant eyeball cell; the DNA of each of these, of each particular type of cell in each particular type of each of the millions of different organisms on earth is unique and different from every other type of DNA in the universe. Second, the DNA molecule must be able to duplicate itself, to form its child in its own image.

What I'm going to say now may be an oversimplification, but I think we can understand the basic ways in which DNA performs its functions as follows:

Just as in a protein, the number and arrangement of organic molecules along the chains which form the vertical sides of the ladder define what the DNA molecule actually is, in the same way that the arrangement of the features of your face define you and make you recognizable as different from every other human being on the face of the earth. And the rungs of the ladder, the bases, are responsible for enabling it to reproduce itself.

There are just four kinds of bases in DNA. They are called adenine (A), guanine (G), thymine (T), and cytosine (C). All the rungs in the ladder are composed of combinations of these four bases. Actually each rung is made of two bases, one extending out from each vertical side of the ladder:

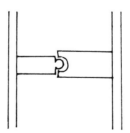

But the bases are particular about whom they link up with: adenine will join only with thymine, while cytosine will join only with guanine. These are the only combinations that will give rungs of the same length, and obviously this is a necessary condition to have a stable ladder (DNA molecule). Imagine trying to put together a ladder with rungs of different lengths!

And this is the key to the duplication process. When the cell wants to reproduce, the double helix of DNA splits apart like a zipper unzipping:

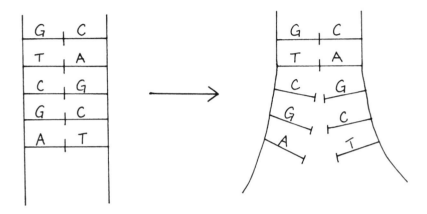

Until finally the entire DNA molecule is unzipped, forming two new molecules—each of which is only one half of the original ladder:

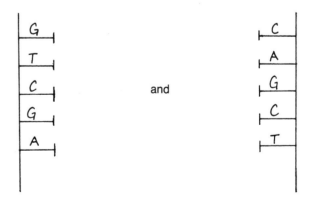

Now what happens next is fascinating. The material in the
nucleus, the *nucleoplasm*, contains all the organic molecules
that go to constitute the DNA molecule, just floating around
there. When a particular molecule with the right base floats by,
it becomes hooked onto the half rung sticking out, and two new
zippers begin to form:

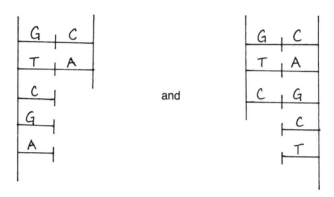

This goes on all along the two separated strands, and eventually the process is completed by the formation of two entirely
new and complete DNA molecules—and each of them is identical to the one that originally split!

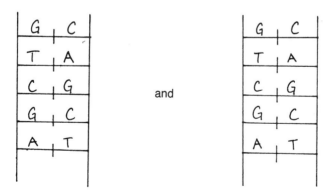

The DNA twins which are thus formed then separate from each other and migrate to opposite ends of the nucleus. The cell splits in two with half of each nucleus going into each half of the new cells, and we end up with two new cells, each chemically and biologically identical to the original cell. So where we had originally one human skin cell we now have two—and they are human skin cells and nothing else at all.

When an entire organism is to be sexually reproduced, this process takes place in the *germ cells:* the ovum of the female and the sperm of the male. These then combine to form a new individual that is not a duplicate of either father or mother, but a combination of the two—and of all their ancestors from which their DNA was built up.

So we each of us are created by DNA, which is a series of combinations of mothers and fathers stretching back in time literally billions of years; we are the unique sum of all that experience. It makes a guy sort of humble, doesn't it?

This, then, constitutes the living process as we defined it: duplication of cells and replication of the entire organism. But there is something else that is necessary. If all life on earth started out as one simple cell, how did it become the complex spectrum of different species that constitutes all life on earth today? There must be something else to life—and there is. It is the ability to *evolve.*

But what does this mean, and how does it work? How did a fish evolve into an amphibian into a snake into a bird? Starting from the first primal cell, how did man evolve?

CHAPTER 11

Evolution, Mutation, and Cancer

LITTLE by little, that's how.

Consider what happens when a DNA molecule unzips and reforms itself. It reforms perfectly into an exact duplicate of the original molecule. But what if something goes wrong?

What could go wrong? Lots of things. Suppose a high energy cosmic ray comes zooming down from outer space and strikes the new DNA molecule—which is, remember, a highly organized structure composed of organic molecules, each of which in turn is a highly organized structure composed of C,N,H,O, and P atoms. The cosmic ray might knock any one of the atoms out of the molecule, or it might even change one kind of atom into another. The result would be that the organic molecule is now *different*—and that would mean that the entire DNA is now different.

Different in what way? That's impossible to tell. But since the function of the DNA (and the proteins) depends on its (their) structure, any change in the atomic structure makes the resulting molecule different, with a different function. The difference might be so small as to be meaningless, and in fact this will be the usual result. But sometimes it could be important.

The resulting cell, the one that carries the malformed DNA,

is called a *mutation* or *mutant* cell. The mutation is a random one; that is, any atom might be affected, and the result might be anything at all. For example, in a stomach cell, the result might be a cell that can't carry on its digestive work. It also might be a cell that reproduces rapidly. If both these things happen, you're beginning a *cancer* because when a mutant cell reproduces, it reproduces the mutation. And so cancer is a widely spreading group of mutant cells that won't do their proper work. If these take over your stomach, you die of stomach cancer. And it all begins in one tiny cell.

The same thing can happen in any organ in your body. And there are lots of things that are *mutagenic* (causing mutations) or *carcinogenic* (causing cancers): besides cosmic rays, there are radiations of all kinds and chemicals of all kinds—particularly the noxious mixture found in cigarette smoke, so that smokers end up with lung cells that cannot breathe.

If the mutation occurs in a germ cell, it can be passed on to the new organism, to the child. If the effect of the mutation is large enough, the child may be significantly changed from its parents. It may be stunted in growth—or it may be bigger, taller, stronger. It might even have four arms and green skin, or be able to leap tall buildings at a single bound. In fact, we have no way of predicting the effect.

What happens next? If the mutant creature has benefited from its mutation, it will grow up and have children itself—and since its DNA carries the mutation in it, the mutation will be passed on to its children. If the mutation is harmful, the chances are that the creature will die before it can have children, and the mutation dies out. In this way, usually only beneficent mutations are passed on from one generation to another, and so the generations evolve into "better" creatures— although the meaning of the word "better" is subject to argument.

This process is happening all the time. Very few noticeable

mutations occur in any human lifetime, almost every child born is a reasonable combination of its parents in the normal manner. But as millions of years pass by, the effects of the few mutations begin to multiply and gradually every organism changes, evolves, and new types of organisms become recognizable; we say finally that a new *species* has been formed.

This process is what we call *evolution*. The accumulated random mutations of millions of years of genetic accidents slowly, in ways not yet completely understood, came together to give new species, new creatures. Thus we moved, over millions and billions of years, from single cells to multicelled animals, from fish to amphibian, from some unrecognized apelike ancestor to man.

And this entire process that we call life, which includes evolution, is carried on by the two types of organic molecules that we have described: the proteins and the nucleic acids.

Now remember that we don't know everything today, we're only beginning to understand the basic mechanisms of life. But from what we *do* know, it seems clear that in order to have life all we need are these two kinds of organic molecules and the proper conditions: a planet warm enough and wet enough.

And we know that if we have the proper atoms—C,H,O,N, and P—and the proper conditions, the organic molecules will form themselves. Remember Friedrich Wöhler? All you have to do is mix some carbon, nitrogen, hydrogen and oxygen together in a beaker of water and they will form ammonium cyanate; and then just heat the ammonium cyanate and it will form itself into the organic molecule urea. Since that time we have made all sorts of organic molecules and—perhaps even more important—we have found them formed in nature under conditions that have nothing to do with life. We have found them, for example, in meteorites—rocks that fall to earth from outer space, and on which nothing has ever lived. We have even observed organic molecules forming in the depths of space itself, under the influence of starlight. All that is needed, obviously, are the basic atoms and a source of energy. This much is quite clear.

The next step is *not* quite so clear. How do the organic molecules take the giant step of sealing themselves off from the rest of the universe with a membrane, of forming a living cell?

We don't know.

We have been able to take the separate atoms and mix them together in a beaker, pour in a little energy, and form them into the same organic molecules of which life is composed. But we have not yet been able to take the next step—to mix the molecules together and create life in the test tube. Obviously this is a more complex and difficult step.

Which means it will take longer to accomplish. Remember, Mother Nature had hundreds of millions of years in which to keep trying until it happened. The earliest life forms we have found are less than four billion years old, and the earth is more than four and a half billion years old. That means that more than five hundred millions of earth history probably passed slowly by, day by day, before the first living cell appeared. During that time the oceans formed and were warmed by the sun, organic molecules formed, joined together, became concentrated, swirled around, and finally—*finally*—there was life.

And if that happened on earth, why not on Mars?

PART III

VIKING

There is no safety in numbers . . .
. . . nor in anything else.

—JAMES THURBER

CHAPTER 12

The Problem

SO LONG as life was considered to be something mysterious and magical there was no way we could even begin to predict how, when, or where it might occur. We on earth might or might not be the only living creatures in all creation; there was no way of knowing.

But with life consisting of a series of complicated but under-standable chemical reactions occurring in and among complex but understood organic molecules, we can indeed begin to speculate on where and under what conditions life might evolve elsewhere in the universe. In fact, most of us now firmly believe that the formation of organic molecules from nonliving sources is a common phenomenon throughout the universe. Therefore the next step seems not only reasonable but inevitable: where the proper mixture of chemicals and the proper environment come together, life itself must begin.

Take Mars, for example.

Not too warm, but possibly warm enough. Nitrogen, carbon, hydrogen, oxygen, phosphorus—none of them as abundant as on earth, but possibly abundant enough. Water, which is necessary as a medium in which to stir all these atoms around, warm them, and breathe the beginning of life into them—well, water seemed to be the problem.

Throughout the 1960s and on into the early 1970s a series of rockets known as the Mariners were sent to Mars. They didn't land on the planet, but they came closer and closer, photographing the surface and making scientific measurements on the atmosphere.

In 1965, the first successful voyage to get close to Mars, Mariner 4, enabled us to determine that the atmosphere was less than one-fiftieth as thick as the earth's. This meant that liquid water could not exist on Mars—it would evaporate as soon as it was formed. When Mariners 6 and 7 told us in 1969 that the polar whitecaps were frozen carbon dioxide rather than snow and ice, it seemed that the case for water on Mars was dead, and so was the idea of life there.

But then Mariner 9 actually came close enough to the planet to be sent into orbit around it in 1971, and some different answers came back. The polar caps were indeed frozen CO_2, but trapped inside them there was a definite trace of water. And then came the astonishing photograph of water-carved valleys on Mars. This was definite proof that at least at some time in the past liquid water flowed on the surface of the planet. At this time life might have evolved there.

And once life is formed, it can be a pretty tenacious thing. We have seen here on earth how life clings to its last breath, beating unbeatable odds, dreaming the impossible dream, not flourishing but simply staying alive and waiting and hoping for better times to come, enduring the most unendurable conditions. In the frozen valleys of Antarctica, in the scorching deserts of Arabia, in the foul pesthole of Auschwitz, life has survived.

On Mars, if life did indeed once form, it might have evolved into forms suitable for existence on the surface of such a dry planet, it might have learned to live with very little moisture.

After all, a bewilderingly abundant variety of life forms flourish in our terrestrial deserts. On Mars life might still exist, extracting water from sources we would never see with our best instruments if they were orbiting the earth in a Mariner spacecraft. For example, water might still exist beneath the surface, and the creatures on Mars may have learned how to suck it out.

All in all, as the 1960s unraveled into the 1970s, the consensus was that life wasn't tremendously likely on Mars—but it very well might just be there.

At any rate, Mars was the likeliest place to look. In other solar systems (if they exist), there might be other planets as perfectly placed in relation to their sun as is the earth. But these other hypothetical solar systems are at incredibly far distances from us. The closest candidate is several light years away, which means we would have to travel at the speed of light for several years to get there—and another several years to get back. And that's the *closest* one. And we can't travel at anything like the speed of light, which is 186,000 miles per *second*. So we're not about to travel to these other solar systems in my generation or in yours.

Within our own solar system, the group of planets that revolve around our sun, Mars is the one best suited for the development of life (except for Earth, of course).

But with Mariner 9 in orbit around the planet, we had learned all we could about life there from photographs and long-distance measurements. It was time to go there, to land on Mars itself!

But what do we do when we get there?

How do we look for life? How do we recognize it? Sure, if you see a beautiful woman walking by—or a four-armed, green-skinned, elephant-tusked *thark*—you know it's alive. But conditions on Mars are not good for life, remember. The most we could reasonably hope for was to find life that had barely begun. And how did life begin on earth? With complicated creatures like human beings? No, we're among the *last* things to form. Life began with simple molecules forming into more complex ones, finally stirring into life as the simplest creatures a universal imagination could imagine—single cells without even a nucleus, at most a few microns in size. Too small to be seen, you see.

Certainly when we went to Mars we'd want a television camera along so that we could look around. And there doesn't exist the scientist with imagination so dead that he didn't secretly fantasize about the first view on Mars revealing footprints! Or even a gazelle leaping over the horizon.

But no one really expected that. What we hoped to find was some form of microscopic life. And perhaps that life would be similar to life on earth, and perhaps not. So how would we recognize it? How could we tell, by sending an unmanned spacecraft to Mars, if there was life there?

CHAPTER 13

The Solutions

WELL, it was a tough problem. But it was the most exciting problem anyone could think of. There aren't many more fascinating ways to spend your days and nights than trying to think up a way to detect life on another planet, especially when you know you're actually going to get the chance to try.

Actually, in the end not everyone did get that chance. As soon as the word got around that we really were going to send a rocket to Mars, that we were going to land it on Mars and include experiments to search for life there, people began to think about what those experiments should be. And our scientific imaginations worked so well and so fruitfully that as the months went by, one suggestion after another came in—and pretty soon it was obvious that there wouldn't be room on the Viking (as the rocket to be sent to Mars was named) for all these experiments.

And so the contest was on. The best chemists and biologists in the world worked for years to develop their ideas into working instruments, and then to simplify them so they'd have a reasonable chance of working when they were more than 200 million miles away, and then to make them smaller and lighter so they'd fit in the very limited space available.

Most of the ideas never made it to the design and construction stage, and most of those that did never made it to Mars: there just wasn't enough room available to fit them all in. Before Viking was sent off, a team of the best scientists had to sit down and evaluate the different experiments, they had to decide which had the best chance of success, of finding life if it was there—and of *not* finding it if it wasn't there! This last condition was the most important of all, because no one wanted to be embarrassed by claiming they had found life out there, only to be proven wrong in later years. This was too important a question to take any risk of getting the answer wrong. When finally they would announce the result of the Viking experiments to the entire world, they wanted to be sure they were right.

So how do you find life? What kind of life could we expect to exist on another world? We know from laboratory experiments that when the normal chemical elements carbon, oxygen, phosphorus, nitrogen and hydrogen are mixed together they will form organic molecules such as amino acids and proteins. And since we know that these elements are about as abundant on Mars as they are on earth, the same processes should take place there: the basic building blocks of life as we know it on earth should also be the material out of which life on Mars might form. But the shapes of those Martian living things would probably be vastly different. Since the particular molecules of living things on earth were formed by random chemical processes, it is not likely that they would be duplicated exactly on another planet. Life on Mars—or anywhere else— must have a different biochemical makeup, and must evolve into different living creatures. We would not expect to see human beings or cockroaches or chrysanthemums or nightingales on Mars—but there is one thing that almost certainly will be the same: life wherever it forms in this universe is going to be a chemical combination of carbon molecules, governed by the same laws of chemistry and physics we know here on earth.

Why? Because no other atom in the universe has the chemical versatility to form such complex molecular structures. Furthermore, carbon is one of the most abundant atoms in the universe: it is produced routinely as part of the normal element-creating processes inside red giant stars, and is roughly as abundant on Mars—and on any other possible habitable planet—as it is on earth.

So while it's important to remember that life on other planets will probably be very different from life on earth, still its basic chemistry will be the same: different molecules, but all formed of carbon combinations in response to the same universal laws. This would be the starting point for our search for life on Mars.

Of course the possibility always remained that we knew so little about life that we couldn't predict anything at all about it: that life elsewhere would be *so* different from life here on earth that all our expectations would have to be wrong. But if that's the case, there's nothing we can do about it; we're simply doomed to failure. If we open our minds completely wide and admit the possibility of everything and anything, there's no way to pin it all down and investigate it. It makes more sense to leave the wild imaginings to science fiction, where they serve a useful purpose, and get down to the work of investigating the most likely possibilities.

In 1964, NASA reviewed all the experiments suggested up to that time and decided to go ahead with a selected group. From among this group the final experiments that would actually fly with Viking to Mars would be chosen. There would be room for three or four experiments. Which among this group would be chosen? Which would *you* choose?

1. *An ultraviolet spectrophotometer.* We said that proteins are the stuff of life, and that they are composed of simpler amino acids joined together by chemical bonds (called *peptide bonds*).

Now hold that for a moment and think about a violin. Two

violins, in fact, and one of them has only one string, the G string. If you play the other violin, you will find a very strange thing. The G string of the unplayed violin will hum in *resonance* with the played violin—and only when the G string of the played violin is strummed. For all other sounds the solitary G string will remain silent. This is because it absorbs the energy of the sound waves created by the playing only when it's own energy level—denoted by the musical notation G—is matched by the emitted sound from the other violin.

The same thing happens with chemical bonds. If you shine light on a molecule held together by chemical bonds, the molecule will absorb the light if the energy levels of the light and the bonds are precisely identical.

For the peptide bonds of proteins, the energy levels correspond to those found in ultraviolet light. So Dr. Sol Nelson of the Melpar Corporation designed an instrument that would shine ultraviolet light on the Martian soil and would measure the energy levels of the light that passed through. Portions of the light with energy levels matching the energy levels of the bonds in the soil would be absorbed, and his *spectrophotometer* would record this and tell him exactly at what energy the light had disappeared. If the light energy matched that of peptide bonds, he could say that proteins were present in the soil.

But there are some other chemical bonds beside peptide bonds that will absorb the ultraviolet light, so a means of distinguishing them had to be developed. And proteins can exist without being alive, so their presence wouldn't prove the presence of life. Of course, their absence would prove the *absence* of life . . . Dr. Nelson and his group got to work.

2. A *mass spectrometer.* When complicated organic molecules like proteins or nucleic acids are bombarded with electrons, they break apart into fragments with definite, predictable characteristics. The mass spectrometer measures the mass of these fragments, and the pattern of masses obtained gives a sort

of fingerprint of the molecules they came from. The mass spec, as we gaily call it, can therefore identify the organic molecules present on Mars. Of course, that doesn't tell if there's anything alive up there, does it? Nevertheless, Dr. Klaus Biemann and his associates at MIT got to work.

3. A *gas chromatograph.* Organic molecules can also be identified by gas chromatography. In this technique the soil is heated and any organic molecules would be vaporized into gases, which are then passed through a long coiled column. Molecules of different size pass through the column at different rates, and as each comes through it is measured and identified. Again, this machine doesn't detect life, it only detects the material out of which life is made. Feeling that that in itself is important, Dr. Vance Oyama of the Ames Research Center and his team got to work.

Well, okay, but what about *life?* Obviously if life is going to be present, the material out of which it is made must be there. But all those proteins and nucleic acids could be there and *still* the planet could be dead. After all, as I said earlier, we see evidence of complex organic molecules being formed out in empty space—and nobody thinks that there's anything alive out there!

So can't we detect *life,* the living process itself?

Well, it's not so easy. How do you tell if something's alive? What is the unmistakable criterion of a living system? Remember what we said before? It's *evolution.* Living things evolve, and nonliving things do not (within a very precise biologically-oriented definition of what constitutes evolution). But how does that help us? It takes millions of years for evolution to produce observable changes in a living population! No experiment can wait around for that to happen.

So we have to find other criteria for the presence of life. We have to be very, very clever.

CHAPTER 14

How to Be Very, Very Clever

WE WANT an experiment that will detect the presence or absence of the living process itself. We want to send an unmanned spacecraft across two hundred million miles of space, land it on an alien planet, have it automatically reach out an arm to scoop up a sample of Martian soil, and then do an experiment on the soil that will tell us unequivocally if there is anything alive crawling around in that clump of dirt.

It's a tough job. A bunch of brilliant scientists sat around and thought and talked and argued and carried out years of experiments, and came up finally with some fascinating suggestions:

1. *The Wolf Trap.* The first idea that seemed likely to work was thought up by Dr. Wolf Vishniac, of the University of Rochester. A *culture medium* is an environment in which bacteria can grow: it's simply a plate of food that they like to eat, sealed off from outside influences. The food that they like consists of a mixture of simple organic molecules, looking like a clear, Jello-like substance. If there are bacteria around they will begin to eat, be happy, grow and reproduce, forming a *colony* in the culture. As they do this, they can be seen as a dark or cloudy patch on the clear culture medium. The experiment Dr.

Vishniac visualized was a simple culture medium with a light shining through it. Originally, with no bacteria present, the light would shine easily through the clear food. As the bacteria begin to reproduce and form a growing colony, they will darken the medium and absorb the light. If one puts a light detector in the package, it will show the light to be dimming as the bacteria grow. If the light doesn't dim, there are no bacteria present. If it does, there are.

2. A *television microscope*. This was suggested by Dr. Joshua Lederberg of Stanford University. The idea was simple: we can see bacteria, algae, fungi and other simple one-celled organisms in the microscope on earth. So simply hook up a TV camera to a microscope on Viking and let it send microscope pictures back to earth. If we see a bacteria there, the answer would be clear: life on Mars!

But there were problems. If there was life, it was expected to be sparse: the soil would be barren, like our deserts, rather than overflowing with critters like the dirt of the Amazon jungle. If you pick up a handful of barren soil and look at it under the microscope, you wouldn't be likely to see anything alive— there'd simply be too much dirt in the way. So someone had to figure out a way to separate the nonliving Martian dirt from whatever little creatures might be there. And how do you focus a microscope or change magnification from a hundred million miles away? Well, you simply use automatic procedures. *Simply?* Well, maybe. . . . Lederberg and his associates got to work.

3. *Gulliver.* This gets a bit more complicated. In this experiment we are looking for creatures that are more like you and me than like bacteria. Not huge, walking-around creatures, of course, but something that metabolizes its food the way we do. When we are fed food (organic compounds containing carbon atoms) we digest it and metabolize it—which means simply that

our body begins a series of chemical reactions in our stomach that breaks the organic molecules down into simpler ones. From this process we extract the building blocks and energy we need to stay alive, and we produce a bunch of waste products. Some of this waste is in the form of CO_2, and we breathe this out into the atmosphere.

That's what we're going to look for in this experiment, suggested by Dr. Gilbert Levin of Hazleton Laboratories and Dr. Norman Horowitz of the California Institute of Technology. They suggested dumping the Martian soil into a kind of nutritious soup. If there are any living organisms in the soil they'll just love the soup and so they'll eat it or drink it or whatever; at any rate they'll begin to metabolize the organic nutrients, and they'll release carbon dioxide (CO_2). Now the ingenious aspect of this experiment is that the organic molecules in the soup will be *labeled* with carbon-14.

Carbon-14 (^{14}C) is a radioactive atom of carbon that does *not* occur naturally in the atmosphere of earth or Mars (well, actually it does, but in very small amounts). When the living organisms in the Martian soil metabolize the soup that they eat, they will breathe out not normal CO_2, but CO_2 in which the carbon atom is radioactive! A Geiger counter suspended above the soup will then record the growing radioactivity as the soup is metabolized and the radioactive CO_2 is breathed out into the chamber. And of course, if the Geiger counter records no growth of radioactivity, then there is nothing alive in the soil— or at least nothing eating the soup.

4. The multivator. This is a series of experiments suggested by Joshua Lederberg, who was also working on the television microscope. The most likely experiment in this multivator series was an attempt to look for *phosphatase* activity.

We burn coal or oil to get energy, which means that the coal and oil molecules have locked up in them a store of energy, which can be liberated by the proper reaction. In the same way, the food we eat also has energy locked up in it, which our bodies are able to liberate.

Both the food we eat and the fossil fuels we burn are basically carbohydrates—chemicals formed of carbon and hydrogen. They are complicated molecules, and in order to form them energy had to be put into them—by compressing them deep inside the earth under tremendous temperatures and pressures in the case of coal and oil, or by plants harnessing the energy of the sun in the case of our food. This stored energy can be released by burning, in which the carbon (C) and hydrogen (H) react with oxygen (O) to form CO_2 and H_2O. This works fine for coal and oil but not for food: we don't walk around with little fires burning in our stomachs (although it can feel that way if you eat a lot of Mexican food).

Instead, we use a series of chemical reactions to release the energy gradually. Constantly appearing in these reactions is one particular compound, called ATP for short (it's full name is *adenosine triphosphate*, which is a lovely way of saying it's a molecule with three phosphate groups, each of them carrying one phosphorus and three oxygen atoms. These organic chemists really do have a sense of poetry, don't they? Although they don't think of themselves as particularly romantic, it's clear that they're made of the same stuff as Shelley and Byron).

ATP and our food molecules interact with each other by particular chemical reactions called phosphatase reactions, in which one of the phosphate groups is lost from the ATP; the oxygen bound in that molecule is freed to react with some of the C and H of the food molecule and energy to keep us alive is liberated—and as a result of this chemical activity we form a *fluorescent* molecule.

Fluorescence is a peculiar property some molecules possess. It was discovered back in the year 1602, when a Bolognese shoe cobbler and part-time alchemist, Signor Vincenzo Cascariolo, while hiking on Mt. Pesara found a heavy mineral that sparkled brilliantly in the bright Italian sunshine. He brought it home and gave it to his wife, who placed it on the mantel in their bedroom.

In the middle of the night Signor Cascariolo was awakened by his wife's screams! And there on the mantel was the mineral he had brought home, shining at them in the dark!

You can understand why she was frightened, but today we understand that it was not the eye of the devil, it was simply a fluorescent mineral—one that absorbs the sunlight and holds it inside, reemitting it later at a different wave-length so that it shines bright green or blue (depending on the wave-length characteristic of the atomic structure of the molecules composing it).

In the phosphatase chemical reaction, which is characteristic of biological metabolizing activity, one of the residue molecules is fluorescent. So it will absorb any light shone on it, and then later reemit it with a characteristic color (at a characteristic wave-length). This forms the principle of the multivator experiment: expose the Martian soil to food, shine a light on it, and then look for fluorescent light coming out of it.

5. *The Left-handedness of Life.* We talked earlier about the fact that the complex amino acids of which life is composed can be compared in their structure to right-handed and left-handed gloves; one of the forms can rotate polarized light to the right and the other form rotates it to the left. When these chemicals are made in the laboratory, or anywhere in the universe by nonliving processes, an equal mixture of both *isomers* is formed: this racemic mixture consists of equal numbers of molecules that will rotate light to the right and to the left, and therefore the result of passing light through it is no rotation at all, since the two processes cancel each other out. But if the amino acids are formed by a living system they are always *levo-rotary:* they rotate polarized light always to the left.

So if organic molecules are found on Mars—which everyone

assumed would be the case—here is a way of determining if they were formed by living processes (as they are here on earth) or by nonliving processes (as they are in meteorites and out in space). Dr. Ira Blei of the Melpar Corporation designed an experiment to produce a beam of polarized light on Mars, send it through the Martian molecules, and see if it rotated or not.

6. *The J Band.* This is not a swing orchestra of the 'fifties, but a kind of compromise between the first series of experiments, which were designed to look for organic compounds, and the second, which were designed to look for life processes. We saw earlier that life is composed of specific organic molecules, proteins and nucleic acids. We can test for them by using dyes and looking for specific color changes. To understand this, we have to begin with the concept of *color*: why are roses red and violets blue? Let me start by asking another question: what color is a rose in the dark? You might think it's still red, although you can't see it, but that's not so. It has *no* color in the dark, because of the very nature of the concept of color. What we call *color* is simply how our eyes react to particular light frequencies. Light, remember is an electromagnetic wave traveling through space, and the frequency of the waves defines the color of the light:

Light of low frequency (red)

Light of high frequency (blue)

The color red, for example, has a lower frequency than the color blue—and that is the only difference between red light and blue light. When you shine ordinary white light (a mixture of many frequencies) such as sunlight on a rose, it absorbs light of most frequencies—but not red. It *reflects* the particular light frequency that we call red, and so the rose looks red to us. A violet, on the other hand, absorbs the red frequencies and reflects the blue or violet frequencies. And that is why roses are red and violets are blue, and if you didn't know this, now you do.

So what color is a rose in the dark? Since no light is shining on it, it can't reflect any light—and therefore it hasn't any color at all.

Now let's go back to the J Band. A dye, as you know if you think about it for a second, is a substance that changes the color of the stuff being dyed. There are certain dyes that will change the color of particular protein and nucleic acid molecules. Many different organic molecules can produce such color changes, but only the proteins and nucleic acids produce a change at one particular frequency (called a *band*, because it's actually a small range of frequencies) of light. This is the "J Band," named after the scientist who discovered the effect, a man named Jelly (honest!). The experiment is simply to mix the Martian dirt, which might contain life and therefore proteins and nucleic acids, with these particular dyes, then shine a light on the mixture and look for reflected light with the J band of frequencies. There are several other distinctive bands being investigated, but all the experiments are lumped together and called the "J Band Experiments" because it's such a snazzy name. Dr. R.E. Kay and his friend Dr. E.R. Walwick at the Philco Research Laboratories are the people responsible for this idea.

7. Finally, I have to mention the simplest idea of all: the television camera. This experiment would simply send a TV cam-

era to Mars (which is not such a simple thing after all, is it?) and turn it on and look around. If we see anything looking back at us, if the horizon is suddenly filled with Indians on horseback or green-skinned tharks or if the sands are covered with slimy crawling beasties, we'll know there is life up there. Most scientists expected any life, if it exists, to be microscopic and therefore not visible with such a simple experiment, but Dr. Carl Sagan of Cornell argued vociferously that we'd be incredibly stupid if we sent up all those complicated experiments discussed above and didn't take the time to just look around and see what's up there.

And that's about it. In 1965, ten years before Viking was sent off to Mars, these were the experiments that were being discussed—"discussed" being a polite word that scientists use to describe the intense arguments, brow-beating, intimidation, and every sort of persuasion just short of outright physical attack that went on day after day, week after week, year after year, until the three or four experiments that were all there was room for on Viking were finally agreed on.

The problem was to find a series of such experiments that, taken together as a whole, would by their results tell us unequivocally whether there was anything alive up there on Mars or not. The experiments that would fly to Mars are among those described. If you were the man in charge, which three or four of them would you have chosen?

CHAPTER 15

Ten Little Indians

OF ALL the great suspense thrillers ever written, Agatha Christie's *And Then There Were None* must be one of the best. It's the story of ten people held in isolation on a remote island—and one by one they are murdered.

We have here ten little experiments, and one by one they were murdered. The only difference between these murders and Agatha Christie's is that we know from the start who the Viking murderers are—the victims themselves. When the Viking program was approved, in 1968, NASA called together a team of about twenty scientists composed of those who had suggested experiments or who had demonstrated an interest and a high degree of expertise in the various concepts involved in searching for life on other worlds. These men, headed originally by Wolf Vishniac and later by Dr. Harold Klein of Brandeis University, set about to kill themselves: they hacked away at each other's ideas, stripping away any false assumptions, exposing any faulty reasoning, examining experimental details—searching for the best small, comprehensive set of experiments that would tell us if there was anything alive on Mars.

And one by one the experiments were killed off. Just as in

real life ("real" in the sense of Agatha Christie's reality) all the murders had a common motive: weight and space. It was going to cost more than a *billion* dollars of your tax money to send Viking to Mars, and there was room in it for just 15 kilograms (33 pounds) of biology experiments stuffed into a box just one foot on a side. Whatever didn't fit had to be discarded, killed off, because no one was going to come up with another billion dollars to send more rockets off.

All the experiments we've discussed were good ones. But some of them weighed too much or took up too much space, or they made too many assumptions or the wrong assumptions about what life on Mars might be like, or they weren't one hundred percent reliable, or the results they might give didn't give clear conclusions. So one by one they died.

The television microscope died, its experimental problems simply too tough to be licked. The ultraviolet spectrophotometer died—but the mass spectrometer lived. It was a versatile instrument that could be used to analyze the gases in the atmosphere as well as the organic compounds in the soil, and so it was too useful to be discarded even though it could not by itself give a positive answer to the question of life. The gas chromatograph lived in *two* experiments: first, Dr. Biemann included the technique in his mass spectrometer to give increased precision to his results, and then Dr. Oyama worked out a new experiment that used it to detect living processes.

The Wolf Trap was killed; for experimental reasons it demanded that the soil be swirled around in water, and the other scientists worried that any Martian organisms would be drowned. After all, they aren't used to water, and probably never learned to swim. This was a contentious problem, and the Wolf Trap made it almost to the day of launch, but just at the end it was killed.

Gulliver survived in the form of two rather different experiments, each using basically the original technique but looking for two different forms of life—and coming up with two quite different answers.

The multivator died, and the polarizer died, and the J Band experiment died, all for the same variety of reasons: weight, reliability, specificity, or some combination of these—or simply because the majority of the group weren't convinced that these experiments would prove once and for all whether anything was living on Mars or not.

Because the worst thing any of the scientists could envisage was that they would go to Mars, carry out their experiments, and still wouldn't be able to say for sure whether there was life up there or whether the planet was barren and dead.

So guess what happened?

Right.

CHAPTER 16

The One-Foot Box

BEFORE we can understand what problems there might be in interpreting the experiments, let's take a closer look at the final experiments themselves, exactly as they were put on the two Vikings that blasted off from earth in that blessed summer of 1975.

First, there were two instruments that were not designed specifically to look for life but would be tremendously useful. The first instrument scheduled to begin operation was the mass spectrometer, which would turn itself on even before landing: as the Vikings settled down through the tenuous air of Mars, the mass spec would begin to analyze the atmosphere it was falling through. This was the first crucial test. For life to exist, there should be on a planet the five basic elements—carbon, oxygen, hydrogen, phosphorus, and nitrogen. And of course there must be water. The result of previous observations from earth had told us that Mars might have a problem in two of these—water and nitrogen.

We've discussed the water situation earlier on in this book. The nitrogen problem might be even more serious: there were no good measurements of Mars from Earth that unequivocably showed the presence of nitrogen, and several theorists (scientists who spend their time calculating instead of doing experiments because they have ten thumbs but good computers) were arguing that because of its small size Mars might have lost its nitrogen early in its history, billions of years ago (nitrogen being a gas not easily held by a planet because it doesn't often chemically combine with other elements to form solid compounds).

You must keep all these problems in mind. When Viking went whooshing off in 1975, nobody really knew if it would find life up there or not. Some scientists argued that it *had* to be there, others swore that it *couldn't* be there, most of us just didn't know.

And this is the most important thing that there is about science: when we don't know something we sit around and argue, sure, but we all know that the only way to settle the argument is to do the proper experiment, to make the proper observation, to collect the *data*. In the case of life on Mars, no amount of arguing or theorizing would ever settle anything, and everyone knew that. The only way to get the answer was to go there. Even then, one might argue about the data, but until we had the data no one could take any arguments seriously.

The next instrument to turn on would be the two television cameras that each Viking carried. This would be the most exciting moment of all. For the first time in history, our eyes would open and look at another world! Oh, all right, we'd been to the moon, but a moon is not a *world*, there was never the slightest hope of finding life on the totally dry, totally airless moon. But here, on Mars, who could tell what scene the cameras would show us? Hordes of native Martians galloping across the desert, tall skyscrapers forming vast cities? A lizard, a snake? An asparagus?

No. Not really. Nobody *really* expected to see anything like that. But maybe, just maybe—? Until the cameras started to work, until we looked and saw with our own (camera) eyes, who could tell for sure?

Anyhow. After the cameras had looked around, the mass spec would again get to work. A long arm with a scoop on the end of it would reach out from Viking and dig a trench an inch or so deep in the Martian soil. It would scoop up dirt from this trench and bring it aboard Viking. The dirt would be heated to about 500° C., and any organic material in it would be *cracked*, or decomposed into smaller gaseous compounds. These gases would be sent through a gas chromatograph to separate them, and then analyzed on the mass spec. The instrument would tell us precisely what organic molecules are present on the surface of Mars, whether they are amino acids or proteins or DNA or whatever.

And then finally the three experiments that were actually going to search for living organisms would begin work. All of these were designed to detect some sort of *metabolism*. This is the name given to the variety of processes—chemical processes—by which living cells take in chemicals from their environment and turn these chemicals into energy, proteins, nucleic acids, whatever the cell needs in order to live. When the cell has used what it needs, it throws out the waste products. Therefore, in all living systems, there is a process of chemical *exchange* with the environment.

For example, we eat carbon-containing chemicals as food and we breathe in oxygen from the air. We combine the carbon chemicals with the oxygen to get energy, and we breathe out the waste product carbon dioxide.

But carbon dioxide is a waste product only as far as *we* are concerned. For other living forms it is *food*. For example, plants absorb the CO_2 and, using energy from sunlight, they convert it back into organic chemicals from which they form their bodies—their stems, leaves, roots and flowers.

The three life-detecting instruments sent up with Viking were designed to test for different effects of this metabolic activity. The first one was called the *gas-exchange* experiment, and it was born out of the early ideas Dr. Vance Oyama had for the gas chromatograph. It was based on the observation that all life, at least on earth, gives off gas when it metabolizes food. Different forms give off different gases, depending on their food and how they metabolize it. I've just mentioned how we give off CO_2 when we breathe, as a result of metabolizing our food with oxygen. We also give off a host of other gases from another orifice in our bodies, although we try not to do it in polite company. These other gases, somewhat more noxious than CO_2, are also simply the natural result of our metabolism.

In the gas-exchange experiment the Viking would feed Dr. Oyama's equipment a spoonful of Martian soil. A nutrient solution—water loaded with good, healthy organic molecules as food—would be introduced into the soil chamber so that its fumes would reach the soil. Any little organisms in the soil would begin to sniff the solution (which was referred to as "chicken soup" by many scientists) and hopefully they would get some nourishment from it. If they did, they would begin to metabolize their food and would give off a variety of gases; chief among those expected was CO_2. Dr. Oyama's gas chromotograph would continually examine the gases in the soil chamber to see if any CO_2 (or any other gases) were given off. Of course, this experiment would have to run continuously for several months, to give the little creatures time to eat and digest properly.

In case the creatures couldn't get enough nourishment just out of the chicken soup fumes, in the next stage of the experiment some of the soup would actually be dropped right onto the soil. The danger here was that the soup might drown them, which is why the fume test was run first.

There would be one final part to this experiment. If a release of gas was actually found, how could we be sure it came from a living process? The final stage of the experiment would be to heat the soil to well over 100° C., sterilizing it—which means killing anything in it that had been alive, just as a surgeon might boil his instruments before cutting you open with them. (There are other ways to sterilize things, but heating them is the simplest way it could be done on Mars.) After sterilization, the entire experiment would be run again. This time there should be no reaction, because nothing would be left alive.

This last part of the experiment is a *control* experiment, and the concept is very important to science. The point is, if you carry out an experiment, how can you be sure it is working properly? The thing you try to do is run a *control*, an experiment in which the technique or the input is slightly modified so that you know the answer—that is, you know what the answer should be. Then if the experiment gives you the wrong answer, you know it's not working properly. In this case, we would know that there is nothing alive in the sterilized soil, and so we should see no gas release. If we do, then we would know that some process other than the one we are searching for—the life process—is giving off the gas, and then we would have to ignore the results (in terms of deciding whether life is present or not; the results might still be interesting in terms of whatever process was actually working there).

Of the three experiments, Oyama's gas-exchange was able to look at the greatest number of possible reactions, and so it scanned the broadest range of possible life processes. For example, if the Martians breathed out a gas that didn't contain carbon, Oyama's was the only instrument that would be able to see it. But it was also the least sensitive of the three instruments.

This problem in sensitivity was because it was looking for gases that were already there. The most likely product it might find was CO_2, and we knew that ninety-five percent of the Martian atmosphere is made of CO_2. So even if nothing is alive in the soil to metabolize the chicken soup and breathe out carbon dioxide, the chamber will already be full of carbon dioxide.

What Oyama's instrument has to detect is not only the presence of such gases, but a *change* in them. And this is harder to do. For example, suppose there are ten billion molecules of CO_2 in the soil chamber, just because they're part of the Martian atmosphere. And now suppose that in the soil there is just one little Martian creature and it belches out just one molecule of CO_2.

Before it belched, the instrument would tell us that there were ten billion molecules of CO_2 in the box. After the belch, it would still say the same: it can't tell the difference between ten billion and ten billion plus one, it isn't sensitive enough.

That shouldn't be hard to understand, since you're not sensitive enough either. Suppose you were looking at a huge box containing ten billion apples, then you closed your eyes for a moment and someone threw one more apple into the box. Would you be able to tell that there were now 10,000,000,001 apples in the box? No way: your eyes just aren't sensitive enough, although you could easily tell the difference between two and three apples in a box. So the question of determining whether an extra apple is thrown into the box (or an extra molecule of CO_2) depends on how many apples or molecules there already were in the box. This problem of sensitivity would limit Oyama's instrument.

The other two experiments grew out of the Gulliver concept. Dr. Norman Horowitz set up his *pyrolytic release experiment* to search for a different kind of life. Oyama's test, described above, was for *heterotrophic* life forms, similar to animals on earth. We animals eat organic molecules and, by metabolizing them, we can change them into the right chemicals to build up our bodies with and also we can extract energy from them by combining them with the oxygen we breathe. Plants, on the other hand, are *autotrophic:* they build their bodies with the food they eat (absorb), but the energy they need they get from another source, from sunlight. Sunlight *is* energy, radiant energy, and

Dr. Norman Horowitz in his laboratory. N.N. HOROWITZ, CAL TECH

by using the chemical *chlorophyll* in the process of *photosynthesis*, plants are capable of converting it directly into the chemical energy they need to carry on their chemical reactions and stay alive. We poor animals don't know how to make or use chlorophyll and so we have to get our energy by eating the plants (or other animals who have eaten plants). In reality, of course, all our energy comes from the sun: when we eat a cow we are getting the energy it got from the grass it ate, and the grass got its energy from the sun.

Okay, back to Dr. Horowitz. He set up his experiment to look for Martian plant-type life. The scooper would bring in some soil and dump it into his chamber. A lamp in there would emit light similar to the light seen on Mars from the sun: Martian sunlight. And now some labeled CO_2 would be brought into the chamber: this is CO_2 in which the carbon atom is radioactive carbon-14. This special radioactive carbon dioxide was prepared in a laboratory on earth, because there is so little of it on Mars that it couldn't even be measured by our instruments there. If any little Martian plantlike creatures (autotrophs) are in the soil they will think the lamp is the sun and they will absorb the radioactive CO_2 and go about their business with it: they will incorporate it into their bodies *because radioactive CO_2 behaves chemically and biologically identically with normal CO_2.* As far as the plant is concerned, there is no difference at all.

After allowing enough time for the plants to photosynthesize the stuff, all the radioactive CO_2 will be flushed out of the chamber. But if there was anything alive in the soil, some of the radioactive CO_2 will now be in its body, stuck there inside the soil. The next step is to kill it (sorry about that) by heating the soil hot enough to vaporize the poor wee thing and turn the radioactive CO_2 back into a gas. All the gas coming out of this *pyrolytic release* (pyrolysis is a chemical change brought about by heat) is swept into a Geiger counter. If there was nothing alive in the soil, all the radioactivity would have been swept out in the first flushing; if there was something alive, some of the radioactive carbon would have remained in the soil and would only now be brought into the Geiger counter, where it would be detected.

So if the Geiger counter sees any radioactivity after the heating of the soil, there was something alive in the soil. If it sees no radioactivity, there was nothing alive there (or at least no au- totrophs there). And the beauty of the experiment is that there is no natural radioactive carbon on Mars, so if the Geiger counter sees anything at all—we have life! (Actually, as with so much in science—and so much in all of life, as you will un- doubtedly see during your remaining seventy or eighty years— there is always a *but*. In this case the *but* is known as the *back- ground count*. Let's not worry about it just yet, though.)

Finally, the third experiment: Dr. Gilbert Levin's *labeled- release* of CO_2. Dr. Levin had started off thinking along the same lines as Norman Horowitz, and together they had been the chief instigators of the Gulliver experiment. But as time went on each of them moved further off in different directions, and they were fated to end up on opposing sides of the final solution.

In the labeled-release experiment, Gilbert Levin (now work- ing with Dr. Patricia Straat at his home company of Biospher- ics, Inc. in Maryland; (next page) sought to detect the same type of creatures that Dr. Oyama was looking for, using the basic method that Dr. Horowitz was using; so in a sense his experi- ment was a bridge between the other two. His results, however, were not.

More about that later. Right now we want to describe the technique itself. He was going to look for heterotrophs and so, like Dr. Oyama, he was going to feed them a nutritious broth and look for any gases they would belch out as they metabolized it. But his broth was different from Dr. Oyama's: he had *labeled* it with radioactive carbon just as Horowitz had labeled his "at- mosphere." In this case the organic molecules that Levin was going to feed his creatures had one of the carbon atoms replaced with carbon-14. If they ate it and digested it, they would have to get rid of the waste products. In terrestrial organisms, the most likely waste product is CO_2, the result of combining or- ganic molecules with oxygen in order to get energy for the crea-

Drs. Levin and Straat examining their labeled-release experiment.

tures to live. In this case, the CO_2 that they would expel would be radioactive, labelled with carbon-14. Not *all* of the CO_2 would be radioactive, since not all of the organic carbon atoms were radioactive—just one per molecule. But that would be enough, because as soon as any radioactive CO_2 was breathed out of the soil, Levin's Geiger counters would see it and we'd know there was life in there.

The advantage of Levin's labeled-release experiment over Oyama's was the tremendously increased sensitivity, since he was measuring radioactive carbon instead of the natural carbon that Oyama was looking for. The disadvantage was its lack of range and versatility: it could detect *only* waste products of metabolism that contained carbon atoms, while Oyama's gas chromatograph would detect any change at all in the Martian atmosphere above the soil (if the change was large enough to be measured by his chromatograph). The difference between Levin's and Horowitz's experiments was that they were looking for different forms of life, and also that Horowitz's pyrolytic release more closely duplicated Martian conditions since he didn't add any kind of soup to the soil. All he gave the soil was artificial Martian sunlight. Levin (and Oyama) thought this was not important; Horowitz thought it would be vitally important. Differences of opinion were beginning to become evident. They would grow, faster than any Martian life could.

These, then, were the instruments that Viking was going to carry across two hundred million miles of space (give or take a bit) to search for life on another world: the television cameras, the mass spectrometer and gas chromatograph of Klaus Biemann and Vance Oyama, and the Geiger counters of Gilbert Levin and Norman Horowitz.

Never before in the history of human endeavor, as someone once said under slightly different circumstances, was so much to be learned from so little—a box one foot on a side, weighing about thirty-three pounds.

PART IV

LIFE ON MARS?

*It doesn't do for people to go about
thinking things. They may get into
frightful trouble.*

—LORD PETER WIMSEY

CHAPTER 17

10...9...8...7...

ON AUGUST 20, 1975, after a two week delay on the launching pad to correct a series of minor glitches that the gremlins inflicted on the spacecraft, Viking I began to pour out smoke and fire, its thunder began to rumble over the Cape Canaveral waters, it shook and it trembled and the solid earth shook and trembled with it until finally it shook itself free, the binding cables fell away, it stretched and reached out and lifted off and blasted away, free of this world forever. It was on its way to Mars. Less than three weeks later, on September 9, its sister ship, Viking 2, sped after it.

Two Vikings were launched in order to do the experiments at two different locations on the planet. After all, if someone on another planet sent a similar mission to earth—to search for life here—he'd get quite different results depending on whether his rocket landed in the Sahara desert, the Amazon jungle, or the island of Manhattan. So it was decided to do the same experiments in two different locations on Mars, to see if the results would be the same. More than two such spacecraft would have been lovely, of course; it would have been great to send a whole fleet of them to land all over Mars. But just these two cost us

113

a billion dollars, and billions of dollars don't grow on trees, you know.

There were a lot of people, in fact, who argued angrily that we had no right to spend a billion dollars on such a wild, romantic fling as searching for life on other worlds when we had so many problems with our life on *this* world. With all the poverty and hunger on earth, how could we explain our spending all this money on Mars?

Well, let's put it into perspective. It *is* a lot of money, it's more than we spend to support our entire National Science Foundation for two years. In fact, it's almost as much as we spent every two *months* bombing Vietnam—and that went on for year after year, ending just a few years before the Viking launch. If we really want to save money for better uses, what we spend on projects like Viking is peanuts compared to what we spend on war, not to mention the money we waste on drunk driving accidents and killing ourselves by smoking cigarettes. We spend—this nation alone—over three billion dollars every year on cigarettes! When it comes to spending money on projects that give us no healthy return, this is a country of experts.

But more than that—Viking *does* give us a healthy return. Even if we had to scrimp and save to send it off to Mars, it would have been worthwhile. Because—look, we've talked in this book about life, about what it is, about what we are. And we said that we are simply organic molecules, proteins and nucleic acids, bound up in our skin like a bag full of water.

But we're *more* than that. We are wild, romantic dreamers; we are creatures of our imaginations. If we have no souls in the chemical sense, we certainly have them in the poetic sense. We started out on this earth, the first men and women, a couple of

Blast off! The Titan rockets lift Viking away from earth, bound for Mars, in the summer of 1975. On August 20, to be precise. JPL/NASA

million years ago as poor, weak creatures: weaker than apes, slower than tigers, less hardy than cockroaches. And baby, just look at us now!

We've taken over this planet, we have been fruitful and we have multiplied; this land is *our* land. There are a lot of people who decry this spreading of one species over all the world, who apologize to the rest of the living world for us animals. But I don't! I celebrate us, I glory in us—because we *are* different, different and *better*!

We haven't become the dominant species on earth just because we have an opposed thumb and fingers to grasp things, or because we walk upright, or even because we think!

We've conquered the world we live on because we *dream*. Because we have had men like Columbus who sail across mysterious oceans to see what's there. As soon as we had the power to build wooden ships capable of sailing around the world—off they went! Columbus and Magellan and Henry and many, many others: Jansz from Holland and de Torres from Spain, Dampier from England and Xavier from Portugal. In the Pacific, far away from our own civilization, the Polynesians built outriggers and sailing canoes and rafts and as soon as they could lash them together they pushed off from their own islands *to see what else was out there.* We are dreamers, all of us, no matter what corner of the globe we dwell in, we are visionaries and dreamers and poets, and the people who tell us of "reality" alone are ignoring a deeper, wider reality that is no less real— the reality of our dreams.

Mars is such a dream. We've stood here on this earth for tens of centuries, all of us all over the world, looking up there

"in perfect silence at the stars"

and wondering, and imagining, and dreaming. Cyrano de Bergerac and H.G. Wells spoke for all of us, John Carter and Buck Rogers are part of us: we want to know what's out there! Our mind, our soul, our imagination—whatever you want to call it—something in us wants to know and to dream, wants to reach out to the rest of the universe and ask: "Is there anyone out there? Hello, out there!"

And so the latest in a long line of human exploring adventures, stretching from the first "Indians" who discovered the continent of America to the early Polynesian sailors to Marco Polo, from the ancient Chinese who wandered north and discovered Japan to Lewis and Clark mapping out our own northwest territories—the latest, the greatest adventure of them all blasted off from the sands of Florida on the longest voyage ever undertaken to seek out new life.

It was a monster, this spacecraft. It weighed over four tons as it left earth, although it would weigh much, much less than that when it landed on Mars nearly a year later. It looked like this:

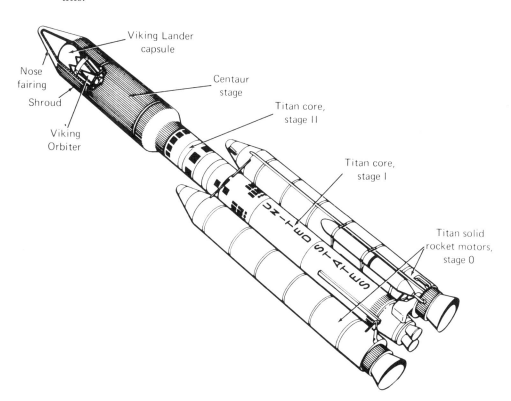

The two solid fuel rocket motors on each side of the Titan core provided the energy for lift-off. They took Viking from its launch pad and burned for just two minutes, throwing it into a trajectory high over the Atlantic, and then they burned out and were jettisoned, dropping loose to fall into the ocean waters. Just before they burned out, the inner core rocket ignited, burning its liquid fuel for another six minutes as Viking rose higher and farther from earth. When its fuel was exhausted, it too was jettisoned, and now the two rocket engines of the Centaur stage took over, driving Viking into orbit around the earth, nearly a hundred miles high.

This orbit is known as a "parking orbit." Viking wasn't really parked there, of course, it was zipping around the earth and waiting for the proper moment—which is a very complicated sort of moment.

Think about it. Look at Mars, go outside and look up at it—or at any other star or planet. Just a pinpoint of light, that's all it is. That's what we're aiming at: a pinpoint of light that's two hundred million miles away! And if that's not hard enough to hit, remember that it's *moving*, traveling around the sun at nearly sixty thousand miles per hour. If you think it's easy to hit a moving target, try shooting at a bird with a B-B gun. (Hey! I'm only kidding.) And to make it even harder, the earth that we're standing on is moving too, moving around the sun just like Mars, but at a different speed of over seventy thousand miles per hour.

So you can't just look up at Mars and aim your rocket there. Because it's so far away that it's going to take the rocket nearly a year to get there, and since Mars is moving along at sixty thousand miles per hour, by the time the rocket gets where you aimed it, Mars won't be there any more! So we put Viking in a parking orbit until the proper moment when it would be pointed at just the spot where Mars was going to be nearly a year later. And then, at precisely the right moment, the Centaur engines gave another huge blast and Viking was off across two hundred million miles of empty space.

Two more parts of the rocket now fell away, their jobs done. The Centaur rockets were no longer needed, for there is no atmospheric friction in space to slow spacecraft down; it would continue on its way, according to Newton's laws, without loss of speed. Along with Centaur, the shroud or *bioshield* had finished its work. This was a shield that enclosed everything that would actually land on Mars, while it was still on earth. Everything inside the bioshield was sterilized, heated to over 100° C. for several days to ensure that no living terrestrial organism remained there to be transported to Mars as a sort of interplanetary hitchhiker. This was obviously necessary, for we had to be sure that any life discovered there on Mars was Martian life rather than something we had brought along with us.

And so the two parts of Viking sailed on, the orbiter that would take up position in orbit around Mars while it took pictures to help the scientists on earth select a landing site, and the lander itself with all its scientific instruments. This book is about the most exciting experiments on Viking, the biology package, but we shouldn't forget that there were a host of other experiments along that were to send back an enormous quantity of scientific data ranging from wind velocities to the chemistry of the surface and the atmosphere, from physical and magnetic properties of Martian soil to barometric pressure measurements and infrared thermal maps. All of these would turn out to be of interest, some of them would be of great interest. For example, one experiment would test Albert Einstein's theory of relativistic gravity more stringently than ever before. A major prediction of this theory is that gravity must interact with electromagnetic waves and slow them down to a predictable degree. In our solar system, the body with the most gravity is the sun—and so Einstein's theory could be tested most severely by listening to radio signals (which are carried on electromagnetic waves) as they come skimming by the sun. Take a look at this diagram.

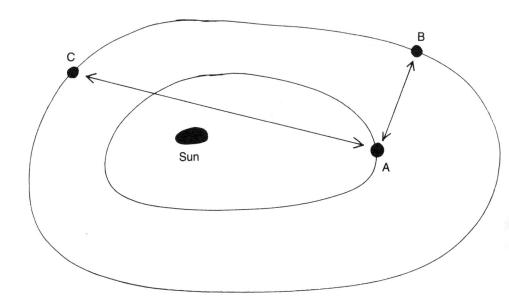

When the earth is at A and Mars is at B, radio waves traveling between them go through empty space and are not much affected by the sun, which is so far away. But when earth is at A and Mars at C, radio signals sent from earth to Mars and back again must slip right by the sun, where they are subjected to the sun's immense gravity. Knowing the distance from A to C, and knowing that radio waves travel at the speed of light, we could calculate how long it would take for a signal to go from earth to Mars and back. Once Viking had reached Mars, then, the experiment was simple: wait till Mars (with Viking) reached point C, then send a radio signal instructing Viking to reply with an echo signal, and measure the time elapsed between sending the first signal and receiving the second. And when this was done, the results confirmed Einstein's prediction that the radio waves would slow down, with an accuracy of 0.1 percent—which was twenty times more accurate than any previous test.

For ten months they sped on their way and then, on June 19, 1976, Viking 1 reached orbit around Mars (Viking 2 didn't get there until August 7). The plan had been for the lander to make its descent to the ground on the Fourth of July, as a kind of national celebration of our two hundredth anniversary, but problems popped up.

As Viking swept along toward Mars it took pictures that showed the entire planet to be engulfed in a dim haze, looking like fog but consisting of fine soil and dust particles swept around by the winds. Then, once in orbit, they took a remarkable picture which showed a fine white cloud in the Martian atmosphere—and the cloud was made of water ice crystals. It wasn't quite flowing liquid water, but it did raise the possibility that liquid water might be around—or at least that it had been there in the past. They all began to be more optimistic about the chances for life on Mars.

But the pictures Orbiter took of the proposed landing site, at the southern rim of the Chryse basin, were disturbing. The land was gouged out with deep channels, which hadn't been visible until the cameras got this close to the planet. It was too dangerous to try to land Viking there, and so they scanned more and more photographs from the orbiter to find a safer landing spot. They decided to go out into the center of the basin, which looked nice and flat like our western plains of the United States.

And then the radio telescope at Arecibo, Puerto Rico, succeeded in picking up radar signals bounced from earth off of the ground in the Chryse basin, and these signals indicated that the ground there was not composed of hard rock. It looked more like sand or dust, and they weren't sure how deep it might be; they were afraid Viking might descend to the planet and just keep right on going—sinking out of sight in a pile of soft dust.

They finally picked a spot halfway into the basin slope on the west side of Chryse, just below what looked like channels that might have been carved by river floods—a spot that looked as good as any they could reach in terms of finding life.

And so, on July 20, 1976, the Viking lander slipped away

Right: A cloud of water ice is seen by Viking Orbiter, floating nearly over a giant volcano. JPL/NASA

Below: The Viking Lander: A diagram showing just some of the experiments aside from the biology package.

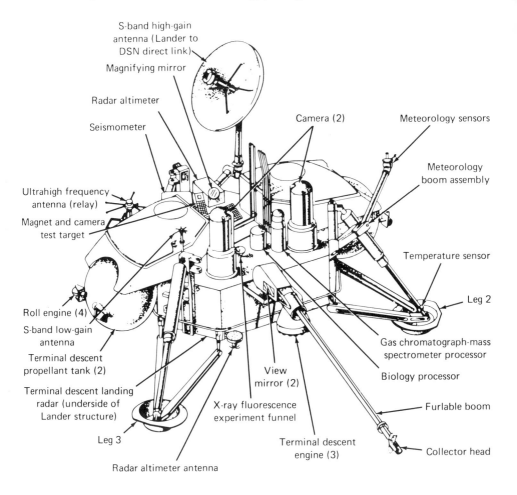

S-band high-gain antenna (Lander to DSN direct link)
Magnifying mirror
Radar altimeter
Seismometer
Ultrahigh frequency antenna (relay)
Magnet and camera test target
Roll engine (4)
S-band low-gain antenna
Terminal descent propellant tank (2)
Terminal descent landing radar (underside of Lander structure)
Leg 3
Radar altimeter antenna

Camera (2)
Meteorology sensors
Meteorology boom assembly
Temperature sensor
Leg 2
Gas chromatograph-mass spectrometer processor
Biology processor
Furlable boom
Collector head

View mirror (2)
X-ray fluorescence experiment funnel
Terminal descent engine (3)

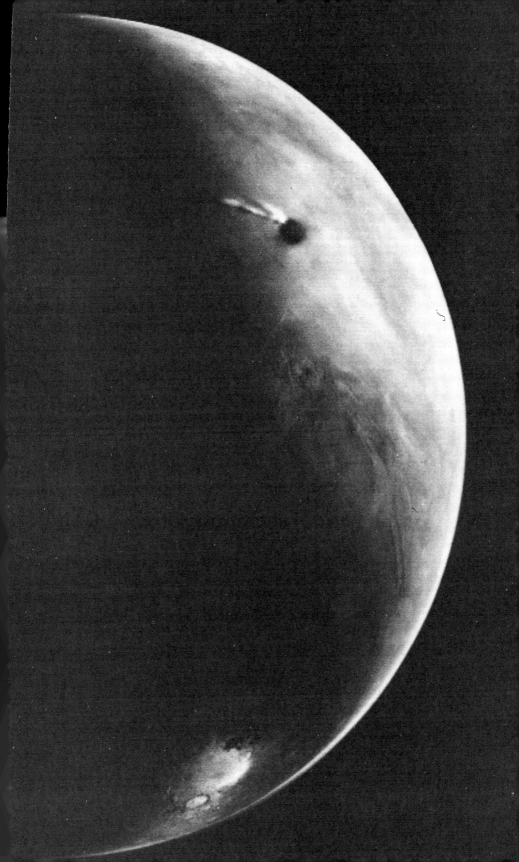

from its orbiter companion and headed down toward the surface.

On earth, the scientists were understandably nervous. The Russians had landed two craft on Mars back in 1971: Mars 1 had landed and vanished without a trace, while Mars 3 landed and sent back data—for 20 seconds, and then it too died. All in all, the Russians had sent spaceships to Mars at least thirteen times, and hadn't yet landed successfully.

Now it was Viking's turn to try.

CHAPTER 18

Touchdown

THE SIMPLEST thing would have been to have a television camera mounted in Viking's nose, sending back to earth the view that a pilot flying her would have had, and have someone on earth fly it right down to the ground as the Apollo astronauts landed their craft on the moon. But it couldn't be done, because of Albert Einstein and the velocity of light.

It isn't really Einstein's fault, he didn't make the rules under which the universe operates, he only told us about them. And what he said about the velocity of light is that it is constant: light always travels at 3×10^{10} centimeters per second (that's 30 billion centimeters every second, roughly 186,000 miles per second). *Always*. (At least in a vacuum, and outer space is as near to a vacuum as we can get.)

We said a while back that light is an electromagnetic wave, and so are radio signals and television signals: they all travel at the same speed. And at the time Viking was set to drop down onto Mars, it was 212 million miles away from us. That means that it would take nearly nineteen minutes for a television signal to reach us from Mars. If Viking flew down toward the surface and there was a mountain in its path and the TV camera in its nose sent that picture back to earth, it would take almost nine-

teen minutes to reach earth. By the time the "pilot" on earth
saw the mountain, Viking would already have smashed into it
(and of course it would take another nineteen minutes for any
command from earth to reach Viking).

So the descent couldn't be made "live." Instead, the Viking
Lander was preprogrammed to land itself, which is obviously a
much more difficult thing to do. On July 20, 1976, just two
hundred years and sixteen days after our forefathers founded on
this continent a nation dedicated to life, liberty, and the pursuit
of happiness, we sent a command across two hundred and
twelve million miles of space and told our Lander to go down
to Mars and see what was there.

Lander heard the signal and popped its nuts—explosive nuts
that set loose compressed springs to push it away from the Orbiter. A few minutes later, when it had drifted far enough away
from Orbiter, its four engines fired up and kicked it out of orbit,
toward the surface of the planet thousands of miles below. For
over three hours it planed on down, its aerodynamic contours
riding the thin Martian atmosphere as a surfboard skims over
the water, slowing it down by friction as it came lower and
lower and the atmosphere became thicker (remember, it is
never any thicker than about one percent of the earth's air). By
the time it had reached an altitude about the same as that at
which our airplanes fly on earth, its speed had slowed to less
than one thousand miles per hour.

At this point a parachute sprung out and Lander drifted down
as it dangled from it, until it was only some four thousand feet
high and falling at a rate of only a hundred and fifty miles an
hour. (It was falling this fast, much faster than a parachute on
earth falls, because the Martian air is so thin.) At this speed it
would crash into the ground and be a total wreck, but at the last

Viking Lander on its final descent to the ground of Mars. JPL/NASA

Lander on Mars. (This is a simulation, of course.) JPL/NASA

moment a built-in radar set told it that the ground was coming up fast and it automatically fired its three terminal phase engines and cut loose the parachute, settling gracefully and perfectly onto the rocky, sandy ground of Mars.

Back on earth, the waiting scientists knew exactly when the

process of landing would begin—just a little under nineteen minutes after they sent the signal. They knew exactly how long the landing maneuvers would take, so they knew the moment at which Viking should be landing on Mars. But they didn't know what had happened—if it had all gone as planned or if there had been an accident—for another nineteen minutes. As soon as it landed, Viking Lander had been instructed to push out of its innards a radio transmitter and send a signal to Orbiter, which would send it on to earth. And just twenty-four seconds after touchdown, a camera on its roof was scheduled to begin taking television pictures for transmittal to earth.

But it took nineteen minutes before the electromagnetic waves carrying these signals could reach earth. It was 5:12 A.M. in California, but the Jet Propulsion Laboratory scientists were all at work, waiting, listening—and then cheering wildly as the first signal came through.

We had touchdown!

Viking was on Mars.

CHAPTER 19

Another World

LESS THAN an hour after the champagne began to flow in the Jet Propulsion Lab, the first picture of another world began to come in and the champagne glasses were held motionless as everyone stared at the television screens. All over America, in fact, people stopped what they were doing to watch as morning talk shows and news shows were interrupted for the first television show transmitted from Mars.

Line by line the first picture came in. The Viking TV cameras, mounted on top of the Lander, looked out through a narrow vertical strip; they started at the top and scanned downward, then moved—slit and all—to the right and began another vertical scan. The transmitted pictures came through in this manner, one strip at a time, until the whole picture was built up.

The first picture shown here was black and white, because color takes longer to transmit and everyone was too impatient to wait. It showed the landing pad of the Lander resting on the Martian soil. The detail was incredible, enough to take your breath away as you sat looking to see the results of years of planning, guessing, working, dreaming, hoping—and praying.

You could see the rivets on the landing pad, which was a great relief. It meant that the cameras were operating with the clarity they were designed for, so that if a tiny lizard or flower were there on the Martian ground we'd be able to see it and identify it without hesitation. The Lander sat lightly and firmly on the soil, which was another great relief, because of that fear that the sand would be so soft that the craft would settle down to the surface and keep right on going, sinking unseen beneath the flowing sands of time, as it were.

The next photograph looked up a bit, scanning around in a panamoramic view from the Lander. This view shows the Martian terrain looking rather like our own southwest desert, sandy and rocky, barren and apparently lifeless.

The first picture from Mars. Notice the clarity: you can see the rivets in the footpad (lower right). It's almost like being there, isn't it? Almost.
JPL/NASA

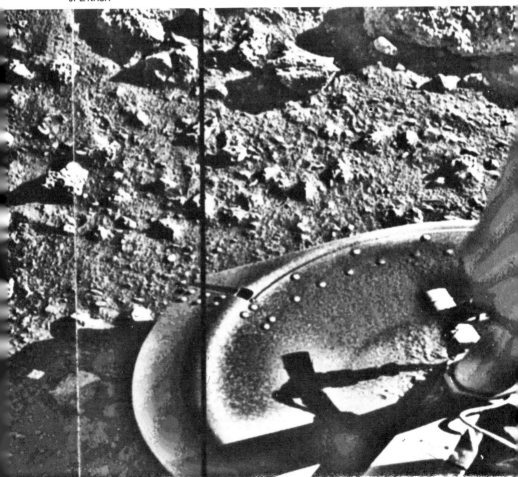

The first panoramic view from Mars, looking up and away from Lander (this shot, in color, actually came on the second day). The horizon is about 100 meters away. Note the several good-sized rocks which could have ruined the mission if Viking had come down on them.
JPL/NASA

There was that momentary tension as the first panamoramic scan built up here on earth, line by line. Everyone, whether he admitted it or not, was staring at the screen and thinking of John Carter, of Buck Rogers, of green-skinned tharks and Martian princesses. . . .

> *Breathes there a man with soul so dead*
> *That never to himself has said,*
> *'What wonders lie in strange, strange lands?'*

And so a collective, barely heard sigh of disappointment swept over America as the camera panned around and showed—not a tribe of Martian warriors, not a half-clad princess, not an antelope or a thark, not a lizard nor a flower, not even a cockroach or a worm. . . .

The sigh of disappointment was barely heard at the Jet Propulsion Lab as it was lost in the rising tide of excitement at what the pictures *did* show. Tremendous relief flooded everyone as they saw the tremendous rocks and boulders scattered about the area. If Lander had come down on top of any rock larger than about a foot in diameter it could have been tumbled over on its side—and effectively destroyed! There would have been no way to get it upright again, and neither the soil sampler arm nor most of the other experiments could have worked. Without any way to get Martian soil into the biology package, the whole affair would have been useless.

And the picture showed many rocks large enough to have done that. How had Lander managed to miss them and come down safely? "Pure genius!" someone shouted, laughing. "Pure luck!" someone else retorted.

It was both. Genius and luck, and a lot more—hard work, determination, careful, painstaking labor repeated over and over again as every one of the thousands of parts in Viking were checked and rechecked, the harvest of many people's sowing.

The initial disappointment at the absence of visible life passed quickly away. Carl Sagan observed that it didn't mean any more than if an alien rocket had come down in our Sahara desert and looked around with its cameras: it too wouldn't see anything alive, while just over the horizon would be Cairo. Gerald Soffen, chairman of the Viking science steering group, said that if you showed these first pictures to a biologist and told him it was a desert on earth, he would tell you that there might well be hundreds of different kinds of living organisms hiding in that soil. Harold Massursky, a senior astrogeologist at the United States Geologic Survey and head of the site certification team that had had the responsibility of finally deciding where to land the Lander, pointed out happily that as it descended its mass spectrometer had worked perfectly—and had found nitrogen in the atmosphere! So there really was a good chance for life on Mars.

But clearly, if there was life there, it was certainly hiding. It would take the full measure of all our scientific sophistication to unveil it and reveal it for what it is.

In the days that followed, a host of scientific experiments began inside Lander. The order of their progression had been carefully worked out before Viking ever lifted off from the sands of Florida to journey to the sands of Mars, the order in which everyone would get to carry out his experiment had been argued over, bickered over, and appealed about and finally decided and set into stone, irrevocably determined. The order depended on a lot of different considerations: the importance, the simplicity, the ease, the chances for success, physical relationships with other experiments, time needed to transmit results—it depended on a host of scientific facets that had to be fit together by the leaders of the mission.

And now, on Mars, they began.

And it was evening and it was morning, the first day. And the second day, and the third day. . . .

CHAPTER 20

The Eighth Day

ON THE eighth day (Sol 8 according to the Viking scientists; the day on Mars is slightly longer than an Earth day, lasting twenty-four hours, thirty-nine minutes and 35.23 seconds. Terrestrial and Martian chronology is therefore slightly unsynchronized) on the eighth day or sol, then, the Lander sampler arm reached out and scooped up a sample of Martian soil. The biology experiments had priority for receiving this, and so they got this first batch as it was lifted up and dropped into the soil entry port. From here it was fed into the carousel, which rotated, dispensing some of it to each of the three biology experiments. The arm then reached out again to get more soil for the gas chromatograph/mass spectrometer, but this time the arm failed. Nevertheless the biology experiments had their dirt, and the three experiments began to run.

At this point things got a bit confused. Well, that's life, isn't it? And life is what we're talking about here. As Robbie Burns told us so many years ago,

> The best laid schemes o' mice an' men
> Gang aft agley.

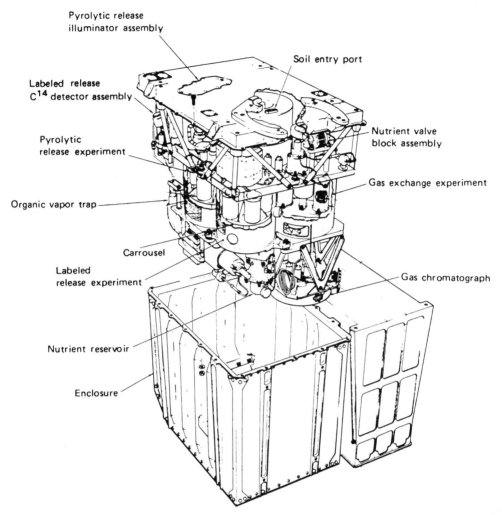

Pyrolytic release
illuminator assembly

Soil entry port

Labeled release
C^{14} detector assembly

Pyrolytic
release experiment

Nutrient valve
block assembly

Gas exchange experiment

Organic vapor trap

Carrousel

Labeled
release experiment

Gas chromatograph

Nutrient reservoir

Enclosure

The Viking biological experiments package

Poets really do know what they're talking about, don't they?
So anyhow, what went wrong with the biology experiments?
Just to give you an idea, listen to some quotes:

July 31 (Sol 11, three days later). At a press conference called
to announce the first biology results, Dr. Klein (the

head of the biology team, which oversaw all three experiments) said that the first results looked "very much like a biological signal," which is a way of cautiously saying that we think there might be life out there.

At the same press conference, Dr. Levin: "The response that we are getting is consistent with the kinds of response we are used to seeing in terrestrial soils (which is due to the living things in the soil). . . ."

August 3, in the *New York Times*. Dr. Levin: "The behavior is characteristic *neither* of a biological reaction nor an ordinary chemical reaction. . . ."

August 4, in the *Times*: "The Viking scientists . . . are leaning toward a *nonbiological* explanation. . . ."

August 8, the *Times* headline:
TESTS BY VIKING STRENGTHEN HINT OF
LIFE ON MARS
Dr. Horowitz: "We have a radioactivity reading that matches the reading produced by algae and bacteria in the soil of a dry valley in Antarctica (on earth). . . ."
Dr. Klein: "This finding . . . does suggest at least the possibility of biological activity. . . ."

August 11, the *Times* headline: HUNT FOR EVIDENCE OF LIFE ON MARS IS STILL A PUZZLE—Search on Mars Puzzles Science—Dr. Joshua Lederberg: "We may not be able to answer that question with Viking."

What was going on? The best biologists in the world had spent over 50 million dollars to design their experiments and

NASA spent another billion dollars to get them to Mars, and now they couldn't make up their mind what it all meant. One day they said it looked like life, the next day they said it didn't, the next day they weren't sure—

As Li'l Abner used to say, the situation was "Amusin', but confusin'."

To understand what happened, let's gather the evidence and ideas together in a series of scientific rounds.

CHAPTER 21

The First Round

THE FIRST round of the biology experiments consisted of each of them simply taking the Martian soil and running them through the experimental routine we have already described. (See next page.)

The results in each case were surprising.

Vance Oyama injected a little bit of his nutrient solution into the sample chamber. At first he didn't inject enough to fill the chamber to the point where the soil would actually be touched by the "soup," so that the only thing that would happen would be that water vapor would rise from the soup and dampen the soil. If the soil has enough nutrients in it to support life—as our own soil does on earth, allowing things to grow in it—then if the hypothetical Martian animals like water, they should wake up and begin to metabolize the Martian soil nutrients—and Oyama was watching to see if they belched out any gases into the chamber atmosphere.

And oh boy, did they ever!

Considering all the conditions of his experiment, Oyama expected to have to wait days, weeks, or even months before the little things realized that there was water there and began to change the atmosphere with their gases to the level that he could see them. But just two-and-a-half hours after he put in his soup, he recorded a tremendous burst of oxygen in the chamber. The amount was nearly twenty times as much as could possibly have been there from any other source except the soil—or rather, what was happening in the soil.

Let's look at this experiment again. Dr. Oyama dropped some soup into the chamber so that the soil was dampened. If there was nothing alive in the soil, he expected nothing to happen. If

Simplified schematic diagram of each biology package

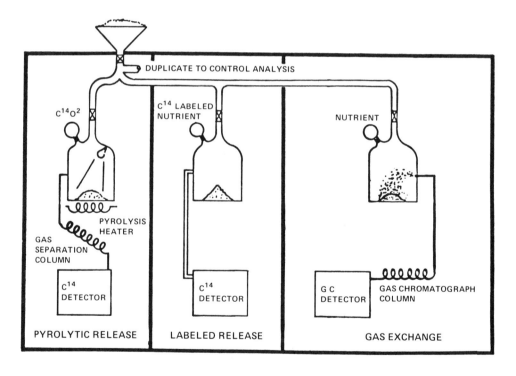

there was something alive in there, he expected that gradually—over days or weeks or months—some small change in the air sealed in the chamber might be observed.

And what happened? First, he saw a tremendous change! So the soil must be absolutely *teeming* with life, right?

Well, not exactly. Because the second point is that the change came *so* rapidly. It takes time for living creatures to eat and digest and expel their little gases. On the other hand, you and I can do all that in two-and-a-half hours, can't we?

But wait, there's a third point. The tremendous amount of gas that he saw was *oxygen*. What forms of life breathe out oxygen? Plants, not animals. Plants take in CO_2 and, using the energy from sunlight, photosynthesize it into organic molecules; then they release the leftover oxygen. Animals breathe in the oxygen and use it to metabolize their food; they breathe out CO_2.

So what was breathing out the oxygen in Oyama's experiment on Mars? It couldn't be little Martian animals, because they breathe out other gases (like CO_2); these other gases were really what Oyama had been looking for, he only saw the oxygen because his instrument was capable of measuring it, and all scientists know that if you *can* measure something you should—even if you don't expect it to be there. This is because we have learned over the past couple of hundred years that many of our most important scientific results were found by accident, by measuring something that nobody expected to be there. This process of accidental discovery is called *serendipity*, after a novel by Hugh Walpole called *The Three Princes of Serendip*, about three guys who wandered around the world making the most marvelous discoveries by accident—something like Inspector Clouseau. This discovery by Oyama is a perfect example.

Because it couldn't be little animals, and it couldn't be little plants either! Why not? Because, unlike Dr. Horowitz's pyrolytic release experiment, Oyama's soil chamber did not have a light source. Without light, plants can't photosynthesize. So what was producing the oxygen? A different form of life, neither plant nor animal? A Martian form of life, different from anything on earth? Could be.

But maybe not.

Life, remember, is just an organized series of chemical reactions. Biology is chemistry, when you get right down to it. Maybe there was some kind of weird chemical reaction taking place when the Martian soil was wet. Maybe Martian dirt reacts with water in a way that earth dirt does not. People began to think about this possibility.

Meanwhile, back at the Lander, the other experiments were going on. Let's talk about Norman Horowitz's pyrolytic release experiment next.

This experiment, you remember, is looking for photosynthesis. The soil is sealed in its chamber under conditions as close to Martian as possible—no water is added, and the light source simulates the sun as seen on Mars. The main difference between conditions inside the chamber and outside—on the surface of Mars—is that Horowitz added some carbon-14 labeled CO_2 to the air in the chamber.

After letting the soil sit there for five days, so that any Martian plants could absorb the labeled CO_2 and metabolize it, Horowitz killed them by heating the soil to 625°C. This heat "pyrolyzes" any organic compounds in the soil and, in fact, vaporizes them—turns them to gas. A stream of helium then sweeps all the gases, including the pyrolyzed organic products and all the leftover CO_2, into a gas chromatographic column. The organics are trapped there while the CO_2 passes through into a Geiger counter which counts the radioactivity. This "first peak" of radioactivity has nothing to do with any life in the soil; it's measured to make sure everything is working all right.

Then the organic products trapped in the column are heated to 700°C, which is enough to pyrolyze them again—this time changing them to CO_2. And now this second burst of CO_2 goes into the Geiger counter, producing the "second peak," which is the important one. Because if there was nothing living and photosynthesizing in the Martian soil, there would be no organic products formed with carbon-14 in them, and so the Geiger counter would see no second peak at all.

Well, let me hedge on that just a little bit. Whenever a Geiger counter is turned on, anywhere in the universe, it always shows a positive reading—that is, it is always counting radioactivity. This is for a variety of reasons: there may be radioactive potassium or uranium in trace amounts in the material of which it is constructed, or cosmic rays (which pervade all space) to trigger it off. No matter how careful you are with your counter, there is always this *background count*, which varies from place to place and under different conditions. On Mars, Horowitz's Geiger counter had a background count of 477 counts per minute. Allowing for various experimental uncertainties, he had calculated that if the "second peak" was between 477 and 492 counts per minute (cpm), he would consider that a negative response; that is, he would feel that he couldn't say positively that life had been detected.

Which means, of course, that if the second peak was *more than* 492 cpm, life *had* been detected.

The result that came back from Mars was, for the second peak, a count of 573 cpm.

Life!

Maybe. At a press conference to announce his findings, Dr. Horowitz said: "The data point we have is *conceivably* of biological origin. . . ."

So the first experiment (Oyama's) gave a positive response, but a different one than anyone had expected. It led people to search for a purely chemical explanation. The second experiment (Horowitz's) gave (in the first round, at least) a clear indication of a biological response, but the scientist in charge was not yet satisfied.

What about the third experiment?

CHAPTER 22

The Third Experiment (First Round)

THE THIRD experiment was Dr. Gilbert Levin's labeled release project. This looked for heterotrophic life (as Oyama's experiment did) by measuring radioactive carbon-14 (as Horowitz's experiment did). In Levin's chamber aboard Viking a carbon-14-labeled nutrient (consisting of a water solution of fairly simple amino acids and organic molecules that might seem tasty to simple organisms) was allowed to drip down onto the Martian soil. While the organisms in the soil ate the food and expelled their radioactivity-labeled gases, the air in the chamber was continually being measured for radioactivity by a set of Geiger counters.

The background count in this experiment was about 750 cpm. If nothing was alive in the soil, the carbon-14 in the nutrient would not affect this count rate. But if anything was alive, the carbon-14 would be metabolized to CO_2, breathed out into the air, and counted by the radioactivity detectors.

Almost as soon as the first drops hit the Martian soil, the radioactivity count began to rise.

After nine hours it had reached a fantastic level of forty-five hundred cpm, and still it continued to rise. Finally, after a week, it leveled off at about ten thousand cpm.

Life!

No kidding this time.

Dr. Levin and his colleague Dr. Patricia Straat had no reservations about their findings. They had designed an experiment to detect life. The signal that life is present would be a climb in the radioactivity count above the background level. They had sent their experiment to Mars. It performed perfectly. The radioactivity count had risen *way* above background.

Ipso facto, as they say in court.

But wait a minute. The tough thing to understand was that the response was such a tremendous one. No one had expected that. A more modest climb in the radioactivity count would have been more understandable—say something similar to Horowitz's result. Dr. Klein focused on this problem at the JPL press conference when he said, "There's no way we can rule out the data as being due to biology. But if it is a biological response, then it's a stronger response than we have seen with fairly rich terrestrial soils and would indicate that microbial life on Mars is more active than it is on Earth."

That would be a hard conclusion to accept. After all, the cameras on Viking had already shown us what the planet looked like. There were no camels wandering around that Martian desert, no little lizards scurrying around—and certainly no human-like Martians were staring back into the cameras and scratching their heads in puzzlement at this alien invader.

We know that Mars is just as old as Earth. If the simple forms of life that Levin's experiment seemed to have detected were as prevalent as they seemed to be—"more active" than on earth—why hadn't they evolved into the larger, more complex life forms we see here on earth?

And why had the response in Oyama's experiment been so large, and so sudden? Why had it been oxygen instead of a carbonated molecule? (Oyama had in fact seen a rise in CO_2, but nothing like his oxygen peak.)

Horowitz's experiment had given the most expected biological signal—but Dr. Horowitz didn't believe that it *was* biological.

So what was going on?

Time for the second round of experiments.

CHAPTER 23

GCMS

THE SECOND round can be said to have begun when the Viking engineers on earth figured out what was wrong with the sampler arm and corrected it so that it could scoop up another bundle of dirt and hand it over to the gas chromatograph/mass spectrometer (the GCMS).

By this time a lot of people on earth were angry and frustrated. They wished they had other experiments sitting up there on the surface of Mars. If they could measure the rotation of polarized light by the Martian organic molecules, for example, that would give them a sure clue as to whether they were alive or not. But this and other experiments that now seemed feasible and necessary had been cut out of the program. One of the principal reasons for cutting out experiments was that we had all expected that Martian life, if it existed at all, would be sparse and hard to find, harder still to measure. Experiments that weren't thought to be sensitive enough to provide reliable results at a very low level of biological activity had been regretfully discarded because of the weight limitations.

But now the results indicated that whatever was up there was up there in vast profusion! Oyama's and Levin's results were

hundreds of times greater than anyone had expected. The discarded experiments might have worked!

This was one of the problems with Viking, and everyone had always known it: scientific experiments are designed on the basis of previous results, and in this case there *were* no previous results. We build up our knowledge of the universe in a step by step fashion, each scientist putting his bricks on top of those put there by others until finally we begin to understand what the building is going to look like. But with Viking we hadn't been able to do that.

We went to Mars cold, knowing next to nothing about its chemistry. The experiments that were sent there were the best ones imaginable—and you can't blame people for failing to imagine the unimaginable.

And, as it was going to turn out in the end, the unimaginable that everyone had not imagined was also untrue.

Because when the GCMS finally got its Martian soil and searched it for organic molecules, it *didn't find any.*

Dr. Klaus Biemann realized the importance of his experiment and checked the results very carefully. He analyzed two different soil samples at each site (Viking 2 also landed successfully, and the same experiments were carried out there as on Viking 1; the results in every case were essentially the same, and so we won't make any distinction between the two missions). He heated the soil through a series of temperatures up to 500°C., by which point any organic molecules in the soil would have been volatilized into gases. These were then passed through the gas chromatograph to separate them, and from there they were swept into the mass spec for identification.

Nothing was there to be identified. The soil gave off CO_2 and water vapor, nothing else, and both of these are inorganic molecules. Dr. Biemann looked more carefully to be sure he had missed nothing, to be sure that his instrument was working properly, and finally he saw a trace of organic chemicals—which he was able to positively identify as coming from the cleaning solutions that had been used in the final washing of the apparatus. The fact that he was able to see these chemicals proved that the instrument was working perfectly.

So why were there no Martian organic molecules?

Actually, scientists (like James Bond) never say *never*, and they never say *no*. They never say that there are "no" molecules present. Because it's always a question of instrument sensitivity.

Suppose I scoop a bucket of water out of a pond and ask you if you see anything alive in there. You look and you see a turtle, so you say yes. Then I take out the turtle. Now is there anything alive in there? You look again and see a minnow. I take that out. You see a bug. I take that out. Now you look and you see nothing alive.

Could you say that there is nothing alive in that water? You'd be foolish if you did, because you probably know that if you looked at a drop of the water under a microscope you'd see all kinds of life swimming and splashing around in there.

It's the same way with chemical analyses. A rule of thumb that smart geochemists have is that "There's a little bit of everything in anything." Nothing is pure. In every ounce of your own body there are some atoms of every single one of the stable elements in the universe, and most of the radioactive ones as well. Yes, there's arsenic in your body, and uranium and radium—but you don't have to worry because there isn't enough to harm you. (Well, that's not exactly true. The problem is that we don't know enough about trace elements and health to be sure, and it's very hard to get money to find out.)

At any rate, the point is that if you try to measure something in a sample and you find there's none there, you don't *say*, "There's none there." You say, "I couldn't find it; its level is below the sensitivity of my experiment."

And that's what Klaus Biemann said when he couldn't find

any organic molecules on Mars: the level of organic molecules there was below his level of sensitivity. The interesting thing, though, was that his machine was *so* sensitive. He could have detected organic chemicals at a level of a few parts per billion, which means that if there had been just a few billionths of an ounce of organics in an ounce of Martian soil, he would have seen them.

This is a much lower level than anyone suspected. Even if there were no organics on Mars there *still* would have been some—because we know that there are organics in meteorites, and meteorites fall on Mars. The low "upper limit" of a few parts per billion was incredibly low—particularly in light of the supposed "biological" response to the other experiments. There should have been many thousands of times more organic chemicals lying around—but they just weren't there. And if there were so few organic chemicals on Mars, how could there be life there? Life is made out of organic chemicals, isn't it? If you don't have the chemicals, you don't have the life. Period.

So what was giving those crazy results in the three biology experiments?

CHAPTER 24

G-Ex
(Round Two)

IN THE first round of the gas exchange experiment, Dr. Oyama had dribbled some of his soup into the bottom of the sample chamber so that only water vapor from it had wet the soil. This had resulted in the immediate release of copious quantities of oxygen and some CO_2. Now, in the second round, Oyama poured the chicken soup over the soil.

If there were really hordes of little creatures in the soil that liked the water vapor, they'd *love* the soup. They should slurp it up and belch out their gases for our edification.

They didn't.

One week after the first round had begun by dampening the soil, the evolution of both oxygen and carbon dioxide had leveled off. Now the chicken soup was poured in. The CO_2 level in the air rose again, but *not* as much as it had before. The oxygen level actually fell!

Again and again, every time someone did an experiment on Mars it turned out differently than anyone had expected.

But each time they did an experiment, they learned something new. Now it seemed clear that whatever was going on in Oyama's experiment, it wasn't biological.

Why not?

First, the results from the first round had come too fast: living things take time to digest and metabolize. Second, they had been composed of the wrong gases: animals don't give off oxygen. And finally, there had been too much gas given off to be compatible with the results of the GCMS.

Now, the results of the second round confirmed this. If there *had* been living things in there, they should have given off more gas when they were fed chicken soup than they had when they were only given water vapor. Instead, they had given off less CO_2, and the oxygen level had actually gone down.

So what was happening?

We're still not one hundred percent sure, but the consensus now is that something weirdly unearthly was happening, something peculiar to Mars.

The rise of CO_2 in the chamber could be explained by a physical reaction that had nothing to with biology or living things. We know that at low temperatures—like those on Mars—any fine, small-sized particles—like the Martian soil— like to *adsorb* certain gases (the gases stick to the sides of the soil). Carbon dioxide in particular is fairly easy to adsorb. So the Martian soil might be loaded with CO_2. Then when the soil was dampened by the water vapor from the soup in round one, the water vapor *displaced* the CO_2: water vapor adsorbs even more readily, so it just pushed the CO_2 off the sides of the soil particles and took its place. The CO_2 was thus pushed out of the soil into the air. In the second round, when the soil was soaked in the soup, this reaction continued—but most of the CO_2 had already been released, so just a little more came off. And when it had all come off, the reaction stopped.

That's not too weird; it's the oxygen story that really boggles the mind. Remember, that's very little oxygen in the Martian air, and it is a hard gas to adsorb on soil, so there couldn't have been much molecular oxygen in the Martian soil samples. (By *molecular oxygen* we mean the form O_2: the form that is the gas we breathe, and that was seen rising into the chamber during the Martian experiments. Oxygen can be part of a liquid, as in H_2O, or solid, as in $Fe_2O_3 \cdot nH_2O$, which is ordinary rust.)

To generate the observed molecular oxygen rise, a chemical reaction of some kind was needed. And it had to be something uniquely Martian, since nothing remotely like it had ever been observed on earth. The explanation seems to be that the Martian soil may contain oxygen-rich solid compounds that react strenuously with water. Such compounds, such as peroxides or superoxides, are known in our laboratories, but they don't exist naturally on the surface of the earth because if ever they are formed they immediately react with the water vapor in our air and are changed into ordinary oxides—with the release of oxygen. On Mars there isn't any water vapor—or very little—and so these superoxides may exist. Then when the water vapor reached them in the first round of this experiment, they immediately reacted and generated O_2. In the second round, it was the "soup" that would have reacted with them, and although the water in the soup would produce O_2, there was also present a particular chemical (ascorbic acid) that is known to *absorb* oxygen—and so the O_2 level decreased.

Well, it's possible.

If it's true, it also explains the puzzling aspects of the GCMS experiment, the lack of organic molecules on Mars. It is well known that organic molecules are easily destroyed by oxygen. We think of oxygen as good for life, but as with other good things—like ice cream, television, sports and parties—it's good only in small doses. Too much is deadly. Because oxygen reacts with organic molecules, releasing energy and destroying them. So if there is a lot more oxygen in the Martian soil than there is in earthly dirt—I say *if*—it would react with and destroy any organics as soon as they were formed. This would explain why there aren't even the organics that we expected would have fallen onto Mars with meteorites—they've been destroyed as fast as they came in.

So the GCMS and Oyama's gas exchange experiments hang together very nicely, without invoking the presence of any biological systems on Mars.

CHAPTER 25

Horowitz
(Round Two)

Dr. Norman Horowitz's pyrolytic release experiment gave a positive answer when asked if life was on Mars, in round one. He repeated the experiment nine times on the two Viking sites and got a positive response seven times (the two negative responses were only marginally negative; overall, this is a definite positive result).

But to be sure, Dr. Horowitz wanted another round of experiments. His line of reasoning was based on the fact that life is known to be severely temperature-dependent. As you know, we all live within a very narrow range of temperatures, and if our environment goes beyond our natural limits we die. We can sterilize a baby bottle simply by heating it to 100°C., by boiling it in water. All bacteria will be killed by this process (and so would be the baby).

This is a typical result for biological organisms: they cannot withstand large variations in temperature. In particular, heating them to 100°C. or greater should kill them.

Therefore, Dr. Horowitz reasoned, let's sterilize the Martian soil. Heat it up and *then* carry out the pyrolytic release experiment. If we get the same result after sterilization that we got before, then the result cannot be due to living organisms. But if the sterilization leads to a negative response, then we would have to believe that there had been living creatures in the soil before it was heated.

He did the experiment twice. He heated one sample of soil to 90°C. This should have been enough to kill most living things in it. Then he carried out his experiment on that soil. He got the same results as before: the 90° temperature hadn't affected anything. Therefore, he said, his positive results weren't caused by a biological process.

To be even more sure, he took another sample of Martian soil and heated it to 175°C. This should certainly have killed the little Martians in it.

And it did. The reaction was nearly wiped out, diminished by about ninety percent.

So were there little Martians living in the soil or not?

Horowitz has pointed out that the temperature of 175°C should have killed *all* the creatures, not just the ninety percent of them indicated by the reaction, and so he feels that his experiment must be interpreted nonbiologically: it should *not* be considered evidence for life on Mars.

On the other hand, inorganic chemical reactions do not usually show such a sudden, nonlinear temperature effect: heating the soil to 90° didn't affect the reaction, heating it to 175° wiped it out almost totally. That sounds like a biological response, which often have such sudden *step-functions*: below a certain point, it doesn't matter how hot it gets; no one dies. But if you raise the temperature beyond that point, suddenly nearly everything dies.

Experiments are continuing in Dr. Horowitz's laboratory on earth, using synthetic Martian soils in an attempt to synthesize the results of the Viking experiment and to explain them without recourse to life. He feels sure that the simplest explanation for all the experiments is that Mars has a peculiar surface that is highly oxidizing, and that gives chemical results different from those we would expect on earth.

But he admits that, until his experiments can explain the peculiar behavior of the pyrolytic-release experiments on Mars, a biological explanation for those positive results does remain a remote possibility.

Only a remote possibility? Does everyone agree to that?

CHAPTER 26

The Third Experiment (Round Two)

LET'S QUICKLY go over the third experiment, the labeled-release experiment, as it was performed on Mars. Carbon-14-labeled food was poured into the soil chamber. Any heterotrophic (animallike) life would eat the food, metabolize it, and expel gases labeled with carbon-14. If the radioactivity detectors mounted above the soil detect any radioactivity, that is an indication of living things in the soil—because for the carbon-14 to reach the detectors it has to be released from the food and expelled as a gas.

In the first round, the detectors did detect such radioactive gases and therefore Dr. Levin announced a positive result: life on Mars. But with the chemical explanation of Oyama's data, and particularly with the GCMS results that there were fewer than a few parts per billion of organic molecules on Mars, everyone began to doubt that Levin's experiment had actually detected life. If a weird, unexpected chemical reaction was responsible for Oyama's results, perhaps the same sort of thing was happening in Levin's apparatus.

And so he too decided on a second round, similar to Horowitz's: he would heat the soil, even sterilize it, and see what effect this would have on his data. And let's go over again what was to be expected if the data were indeed the result of living organisms in the Martian soil: a rise in temperature would begin to kill some of them, and so the reaction should begin to fall off. By the time he sterilized the soil, heated it over 100°C, *all* the wee beasties should be dead and the reaction should cease.

And so the second round of the third experiment began.

Step 1: the Martian soil was heated to 46°C for three hours. Then the nutrient soup was added to it. The radioactivity detectors, which had been ticking along at their accustomed background rate, began to rise—but not as far as they had before! The same reaction took place—radioactive gases were given off—but only about *half* as much radioactivity was generated this time. This was just what would have been expected: the poor little things in the soil were being killed by the high temperature, but some of them survived and greedily lapped up the soup.

So on to Step 2: this time the Martian soil was heated to 160°C for three hours. After such a heating, nothing should be left alive in it. Then the nutrient soup was added, and the radioactivity detectors sent their results back to earth. Before the addition of the soup, they ticked away merrily at their usual background rate. And then the soup was added—and nothing happened. The detectors showed *no rise in radioactivity*!

This was a positive response *par excellence.*

It was exactly what had been predicted if Levin's results had been due to biology.

So Viking discovered life on Mars!

Or did it?

Listen to:

Dr. Klaus Biemann: "The majority of scientists believe that the biology experiments were negative."

Dr. Alexander Rich (biologist from MIT): "We failed to demonstrate that life is there, but we didn't disprove it. It's a matter of judgement."

Dr. Norman Horowitz: "Those areas on Mars examined by the two spacecraft are not habitats of life."

Dr. Gilbert Levin: "If you look objectively at the data, it's more likely than not that we discovered life."

Who's right? Who's wrong? Who knows what life lurks in the soil of Mars? Perhaps only the Shadow knows. . . .

Certainly Levin's labeled-release experiment gave the clearest indication of life on Mars, but there were two main objections to it. First, Oyama's experiment showed equally clearly that something weird and chemical was happening on Mars. So perhaps Levin's results were also being influenced by the mysterious Martian chemistry.

Well, okay, perhaps. But it's now many years later, and hosts of scientists have been playing around on earth with all possible kinds of synthetic Martian soil, trying to come up with an explanation of chemistry that would explain both Oyama's and Levin's results. In 1979, for example, the prestigious *Journal of Molecular Evolution* devoted an entire issue to the question of the Viking biological results, with many reports of scientific experiments and calculations attempting to explain the "biological response" by chemical reactions alone. Several of these were able to mimic the labeled-release effects in some way, but none of them in every way. In particular, no one was successful in explaining the heat sensitivity of the Martian soil by chemical means.

So perhaps different things were happening in Oyama's and Levin's experiments. Oyama's results were almost certainly chemical, but that doesn't mean that Levin's were.

The second objection is a tougher one: the results of the GCMS experiment, which showed no indication of the presence of organic molecules on Mars. Everyone agrees that you can't have life without organic chemistry, so if there are no organic molecules on Mars there just *has* to be another explanation for Levin's results.

And then, in 1981, Levin and Straat reported a new result.

CHAPTER 27

The Third
Experiment
(Round Three)

ROUND THREE of the third experiment took place on earth, long after the Viking mission was over. For five years Levin and Straat had been searching for an answer to that most puzzling of questions: how can you have life without organics? How could their experiment have given a positive result if the GCMS had provided a negative one?

They found what might be the answer in a sample of soil from Antarctica, the ice-covered continent that covers the South Pole of the earth. The temperatures in the *dry valleys* there never rise above the freezing point of water (0°C), and so all water there is solid ice; these dry valleys are among the coldest and driest spots on earth. And what does that sound like? Cold and dry? It sounds just like Mars.

Indeed, these Antarctic soils had long been recognized as being the closest terrestrial analogues to the surface of Mars, and most Viking experiments had been tested on them. From these tests Levin and Straat found a possible answer to the problem.

Antarctica is not a pleasant habitat for life, but things do live there. Despite the dryness, despite the constant cold, the Antarctic soils contain a very low but definite level of microbial

163

life. When one of these soils had been tested by the labeled release experiment, the presence of that life was clearly seen: the
radioactivity detectors showed a response similar to those obtained on Mars. But when that same soil was tested by the
GCMS, it showed a negative response! That is, there was such
a low level of organic molecules there that the GCMS couldn't
see them; it wasn't sensitive enough.

And so Gilbert Levin and Patricia Straat concluded that the
discrepant results on Mars are probably just what they are on
earth—the result of the different sensitivities of the two experiments. As far as they are concerned, their experimental results
on Mars "satisfy the criteria established for a biological
response."

Period. End of story.

And then, there's the Fourth Experiment. . . .

CHAPTER 28

The Fourth Experiment

YOU DIDN'T expect a chapter with this title, in a book with this title, did you? But there was a fourth experiment.

Remember the cameras on Viking? When the Viking Landers sat down on Mars, the first search for life began with those first pictures. We all sat glued to our television sets as the pictures came in, looking for something that looked like a tree or a flower, looking for something that moved, for something that bloomed, for something that changed color with the seasons. . . .

And we saw nothing. Even Carl Sagan, who had championed the search for large, visible forms of life, had to admit after a careful study of the pictures over a long period of time that nothing in them had "obviously jumped up and moved around."

But something in them *did* change color.

It's not easy to see, but take a look at the back of the jacket and page 166. There's a slight green patch on the rock in the middle of the left-hand picture. This picture was taken on Sol 128.

The right hand picture is of the same rock, taken on Sol 615, about half a Martian year later. The lighting is different, so it's

Lichen on Mars? (See text) G. LEVIN, BIOSPHERICS, INC.

hard to be sure, but doesn't it look as if the green patch is smaller *and has moved?*

Levin and Straat, together with Dr. William Benton of the Jet Propulsion Laboratory, have gathered a collection of such pictures and suggested that—although the changes in color pattern and position of these patches on several Martian rocks could have been done by the Martian wind blowing dirt around—they really look more like the form of life we know on earth as *lichens.*

Lichens are among the most ancient and hardy forms of life on earth, possibly the terrestrial form best adapted for life on Mars. When you get down to such simple forms of life, the old distinction between plants and animals begins to fade away, although in most of its characteristics the lichens are best described as plants. What they really are, however, is a *symbiosis* of fungus and alga. The word symbiosis comes from a Greek word meaning to live together; in biology it refers to two different and distinct organisms living together intimately in order to benefit each other. You might think of marriage as being a symbiotic relationship if you think that men and women are really different. In the case of the lichens there isn't any doubt: fungi and algae are quite distinctly different forms of life. But when they form a lichen they live together comfortably, the fungus providing protection for the alga and the alga providing the food for the fungus.

Among their fascinating characteristics is one that appeals directly to the person looking for a model of Martian life: they don't need liquid water, they are capable of using water derived strictly from atmospheric vapor. And they are often found on earth growing on, clinging to, the same kind of rocks seen on Mars in the illustration on page 132.

CHAPTER 29

The Answer

So WHAT'S the answer? Do we have life on Mars?

I don't know.

Let's rephrase the question: Have we discovered life on Mars?

No. We have not. To discover something means to make an observation that *proves* that the something exists. When whoever it was that discovered America did so, there was no question that the land he (they? she? it?) saw really existed. The important word in the definition of "discover" is the word *proves*.

But what constitutes proof? It's the whole basis of what we think of as science. Science is partly conjecture and partly doubt: we sit around and think up good ideas, and other scientists listen to them and doubt them. But if that's all there is to it, science wouldn't be any more useful than an old politicians' debating society; science wouldn't have come up with a cure for syphilis and a preventative for polio, it would never have discovered the origin of the universe or the age of the earth or how the ocean floors opened, if all scientists did were talk to and doubt each other.

They have to go out and dig up *proof.*

Let's say you come up with a good scientific idea, and I think it's nonsense. There's no point in us sitting here shouting at each other; if we're scientists, you'll go out and try to prove you're right and I'll work hard to prove you're wrong. Sooner or later, one of us will get his proof, and then the question will be settled.

Or will it?

I mentioned earlier in this book that one of the Viking experiments measured the time it took radio waves to travel between Mars and the earth, going around the sun, and that the results "proved" Einstein's theory of relativistic gravity to be correct to within 0.1 percent. Does this mean that his theory is now absolutely proven to be right?

Not exactly.

The question is, what constitutes "proof"? And there's no clear-cut answer to that question. I think the best we can do is go along with the legal definition: if you commit a murder, they'll have to prove you did it "beyond a reasonable doubt."

I like that expression: beyond a reasonable doubt. It doesn't define what we mean by "reasonable," it leaves that up to each individual to decide. And it accepts the fact that nothing can be proven absolutely. But if a group of people are gathered together who agree to face the issue squarely and decide it on the basis of the evidence, without regard to their prejudices or previous notions, and if the D.A. convinces them that you're guilty so that they no longer have any reasonable doubt—then I think we have to go along with their decision: we have to hang you. Because if we wait until things are proven *absolutely*, with no possible doubt at all, we'll be sitting around listening to the evidence for a long, long time. (So maybe jail is better than the death penalty?)

There's one big difference between the law and science: in science we don't pick our jury blindfolded from a pool of citizens, we pick them on the basis of their intelligence, knowledge, and experience. It's a much better system, it ensures that we get people who know and care about the business at hand, and yet people who are trained to judge fairly. And sometimes it even works. (As in law operating in a free country, every criminal [scientist] is free to say the jury is wrong when it finds him guilty [wrong]).

In this case, in the question of life on Mars, the jury is still out. The NASA scientists and other scientists at universities and laboratories all over the country have not reached an unqualified consensus. Some are convinced that there is no life on Mars, most think that life has not yet been demonstrated to be there, and some think we have seen good evidence for it in the labeled-release experiment and perhaps in the photos of changing colors on the Martian rocks.

We can summarize the jury's opinion so far in Table 3.
So where does that leave us? Is there life?
It's time for the Fifth Experiment.

Table 3. Is There Life on Mars?

JUROR	Round One	Round Two	"Final"*
Oyama	No (?)	No (!)	No!
Horowitz	?	No	No!
Levin	?	Yes (?)	Yes
Consensus of most scientists	?	No (?)	No (?????)

*"Final" means their opinion as of January, 1984, as interpreted by me by reading their published papers or their letters, or by talking to them, or by omphaloskepsis.

CHAPTER 30

The Fifth Experiment

WE HAVE to go back to Mars.

We went there the first time, in Viking 1 and 2, with very little knowledge of what the planet was like. And if Viking didn't send us back the answer to the question of life, it certainly did provide us with a lot of information. We now know what the atmosphere and the ground are composed of, we have an upper limit to the concentration of organic molecules, we have strong indications of superoxidants and weird chemical effects. We have a better idea of what is there and so we have a better idea of what to look for next. Dr. Levin, for example, feels he could remove any ambiguity from his labeled-release experiment with a more elaborate form of the same equipment, making just a few changes.

No, there's no reason for disappointment in the results of the Viking experiments. They're a perfect illustration of the way science works. We get an idea, we set out to prove it or disprove it—and the experiments we designed don't work out quite the way they were supposed to. We end up not getting an answer to the question we asked, but we find out something else; and that allows us to ask better questions next time, more sophisticated questions that need more sophisticated experiments—and that's the way science progresses.

So don't be disappointed that we don't know if there's life on Mars. We'll go back there again some day when there's enough money, and when we do we'll find out more and more about that mysterious planet . . . and about the mysterious thing we call life. In the meantime we'll be working up new experiments that will undoubtedly provide us with more surprises.

L'ENVOI

"Beauty is truth, truth beauty—that is all
Ye know on earth, and all ye need to know."

Ode on a Grecian Urn
—JOHN KEATS

Suggestions for Further Reading

FICTION

RAY BRADBURY, *The Martian Chronicles*. A pre-Viking novel about life on Mars. Poetic, haunting, lovely. We know now (from Viking) that its hypothesis about life there is wrong, but Keats is wrong, too—so enjoy it.

EDGAR RICE BURROUGHS. Any of the John Carter novels, but the earlier are the best. They all have Mars in the title, and begin with *A Princess of Mars* (original title was *Under the Moons of Mars*). While you're at it, you might try the first *Tarzan* novel, too: *Tarzan of the Apes*.

BUCK ROGERS and FLASH GORDON. The comic strips are better than the books. If you're lucky, you'll find the old ones reprinted. Remember, what some people think about wines is true about Buck Rogers, Flash Gordon, and sophisticated women: the older the better.

H.G. WELLS, *War of the Worlds*. The novel that started it all, and still one of the best.

NONFICTION

S.F. COOPER, JR. *The Search for Life on Mars*. and D.L. CHANDLER, *Life on Mars*. Two books on the same topic as this one, but with a totally different viewpoint. Not as good as this book, of course, but still very good. You'll enjoy them.

SAMUEL GLASSTONE, *The Book of Mars*. An excellent book, at a much higher technical level than this one. A scientific look at Mars and the chances for life there, written before Viking. You'll have to ask your librarian for this one.

JEFF ROVIN, *Mars!* An interesting book with lots of pictures, at about the level of this book.

CARL SAGAN, *Other Worlds, The Cosmic Connection, The Dragons of Eden*, and *Broca's Brain*. Mind-boggling science and speculation.

JOURNALS

N.H. HOROWITZ, "The Search For Life on Mars," published in *Scientific American*, July, 1978. Written by one of the Viking investigators, it is an excellent account of his work and point of view.

Science, Volume 194, November 19, 1976, pages 819–820. This is a magazine written for scientists, and this article is the summary of the Mars Viking biological investigations. See if you've learned enough from this book to understand it.

Index